Design Basics

Cover: Warren Seelig. *Aruba.* 1983. Cotton, aluminum paint, warp face grosgrain, 4′2″ × 4′4″
(1.27 × 1.32 m). Robert Pfannebecker Collection, Lancaster, PA.

Design Basics

Second Edition

David A. Lauer
College of Alameda, Alameda, California

Holt, Rinehart and Winston, Inc.

Fort Worth   Chicago   San Francisco   Philadelphia   Montreal   Toronto
London   Sydney   Tokyo

For David A. Ittner
1963–1980

PUBLISHER
Susan Katz

EDITOR
Karen Dubno

PICTURE EDITOR
Joan Scafarello

SENIOR PICTURE RESEARCHER
Sybille Millard

SENIOR PROJECT EDITOR
Françoise Bartlett

DESIGN SUPERVISOR
Gloria Gentile

SENIOR PRODUCTION MANAGER
Nancy Myers

DESIGNER
Arthur Ritter

Library of Congress Cataloging in Publication Data
Lauer, David A.
    Design basics.
    Bibliography: p. 240
    Includes index.
    1. Design.   I. Title.
NK1510.L38   1985   745.4   84-12861

0-03-063911-5

Printed in the United States of America

    9012   039   9   8   7

Holt, Rinehart and Winston, Inc.
The Dryden Press
Saunders College Publishing

Composition and separations: York Graphic Services, Inc.
Printing and binding: R. R. Donnelley & Sons Co.

Preface

The Preface to the first edition of *Design Basics* stated its purpose as

an introductory text for studio classes in two-dimensional design. It presents the fundamental elements and principles of design—as they relate to drawing, painting, and the graphic arts—in a flexible format that lends itself to many different teaching approaches.

This is still precisely the aim of the second edition, and yet this book is quite different in many ways. It is always intriguing to have another chance at any project. No matter how much personal satisfaction initially greets the publication of a book, second thoughts inevitably linger. Now, with several years of "second-guessing," I felt that certain areas could be improved. Observing the reactions of students, and availing myself of the invaluable help of many instructors who also use the text, I sensed some changes were apparent and desirable.

The most striking change is in Chapter 10 on color. The chapter has been greatly enlarged, to include the area of *value* and to examine additional aspects of color. Many new color reproductions add greatly to this chapter's presentation. Another important change is the addition of a final chapter on design problem solving. This new material attempts to bridge the gap between theory and practice in the studio.

Actually, there are numerous changes throughout the text. Many sections have been reorganized for greater clarity and a number of illustrations changed. Several new topics are also introduced. Since, economically, the book should not grow in size, this entailed cuts elsewhere. Thus, some longer discussions have been shortened, but little material has been deleted entirely. But this is the essence of the book: Many topics are succinctly introduced; each instructor can then decide the areas that need more examples and discussion. No text *replaces* the instructor; the aim is to *assist* in the best way possible.

Amid the changes, however, I believe the positive features of the first edition remain. Foremost is the modular layout, which enables art instructors to determine their own sequence of topics. While about a third of the images are new, an attempt was made to retain the same wide variety of examples that illustrate these basic ideas as indicative of every medium, period, and geographical area. More three-dimensional examples have been included, especially in Chapter 8 on shape/volume. An attempt was made to include less often seen examples, including work by women artists who in many texts have not received due recognition.

Working on this revision has been a challenging but satisfying experience. While hardly an impartial observer, I believe you will be using a greatly improved book.

ACKNOWLEDGMENTS

How can one acknowledge all of the people who assisted in the long process of writing a book? It's impossible, but I must give special thanks to Ernest B. Ball, Helen-Louise Ittner, Margaret Carpenter, and James E. Jewell for their specific help and constant encouragement. The reviewers who thoughtfully considered endless pages of material and made so many good suggestions are certainly to be thanked: Doree Freidenrich, Orange Coast College; Darlene Swaim, Mesa Community College; Ronald W. Thomas, St. Louis Community College; Betty Jo Troeger, Florida State University; and William C. Zwingelberg, Catonsville Community College.

I also am grateful to the many instructors who took the time to write and informally offer suggestions on specific parts of the first edition.

Finally, I acknowledge my debt to the staff at Holt, Rinehart and Winston, the people who made this book possible. Their names may not be on the cover, but they truly "created" this book. I cannot list all that I owe to my editor, Karen Dubno. I thank her not only for her obvious skill and expertise but for her endless patience in resolving problems. Also to be recognized are Françoise Bartlett for her project editorial skills, which turned a manuscript into a book; Gloria Gentile, who supervised the design layout; Nancy Myers for ensuring quality production and printing; and Sybille Millard for her persistence in locating and organizing the illustrations.

D. A. L.

San Francisco, California
September 1984

Contents

Contents

Design Basics

1

Unity

Unity, the presentation of a unified image, is perhaps as close to a "rule" as art approaches. Unity implies that a congruity or agreement exists among the elements in a design; they *look* as though they belong together, as though some visual connection beyond mere chance has caused them to come together. Another term for the same idea is *harmony.* If the various elements are not harmonious, if they appear separate and/or unrelated, your pattern falls apart and lacks unity.

Example **a** illustrates the idea. When we first look at the elements in this design, we immediately see that they are all somewhat similar. Despite obvious differences (especially size), they all have some basic visual characteristics that tend to relate them to each other. This harmony, or unity, is not merely our recognizing all of the elements as "forks." If we had never before seen a fork, knew nothing of the various uses for this tool, or even had no name for this implement, we would still see the *visual* similarity between them all. They are related *visually* because of similarities in shape, and this provides a concept of unity.

The relief sculpture in **b** shows this same idea in abstract terms, using shapes that have no literal meaning to the viewer. In looking at the three panels, we quickly recognize that all of them contain the same half-circle shapes. As with the forks, different sizes are obvious, but the shape remains consistent. The arrangement of these elements varies in each panel, but our sensing the similarity of shapes relates the three together in a coherent pattern. As the title of the sculpture states, an underlying *theme* is presented in several different ways as *variations.* This is the essence of the concept of unity.

The designer's job in creating unity is not necessarily difficult. In fact, the viewer *looks* for some organization, something to unify the different elements. The viewer does not *want* to see unrelated chaos. As the designer, you must provide some clues, but the viewer is already searching for some coherent unity. In creating unified designs, your task starts with picking the elements you wish to combine, but the challenge is truly more in the organization of elements into a composition. Your idea or theme, or even absence of one, does not limit you. The artistic skill of organization (or *design*) produces a unified pattern.

a The units of this design have characteristics in common, despite obvious differences in appearance.

b Barbara Hepworth. *Maquette, Theme and Variations.* 1970. Bronze, 11⅜ × 26⅛" (29 × 66 cm).

a

b

Unity

An important aspect of visual unity is that the whole must be predominant over the parts; you must first see the *whole* pattern before you notice the individual elements. Each item may have a meaning and certainly add to the total effect, but the viewer must first see the pattern as a whole, rather than simply a collection of unrelated bits and pieces.

This concept differentiates a design from the usual scrapbook page, such as the one in **a**. In a scrapbook, each item is meant to be observed and studied individually, to be enjoyed and then forgotten as your eye moves on to the next souvenir. The result may be interesting, but it is not a unified design.

Do not confuse *intellectual unity* with *visual unity*. Visual unity denotes some harmony or agreement between the items that is apparent to the *eye*. To say that a scrapbook page is "unified" because all the items have a common theme (your family, your wedding, your vacation at the beach) is unity of *idea*—that is, a conceptual unity not observable by the eye. A unifying *idea* will not necessarily produce a unified pattern.

In **b** the scrapbook items have been organized so that we are aware first of the total pattern they make together, and then we begin to enjoy the items separately. Example **b** is a unified design. Here, as is often the case in creating a design, the actual elements chosen are less important than what the artist does with them.

The need for visual unity does not deny that there also can be an intellectual pleasure in design. Many times the task of the designer is finding visual symbols to convey an *idea*. Now the visual unity function is important along with the intellectual "reading" of the design. The poster in **c** shows this dual appreciation. The unity results from the repeating horizontal bands of lettering that unexpectedly curve downward on the right side. Then, intellectually, we realize these lines of type are giving us an abstract image of Frank Lloyd Wright's famous building (**d**). The combination of idea and visual symbol is superb.

a If a pattern does not have unity, it remains simply a collection of fragments.
b Organizing the different units into a pattern results in a coherent design.
c Poster advertising free Tuesday evenings at the Solomon R. Guggenheim Museum, New York (sponsored by Mobil Corporation). Designed by Chermayeff & Geismar Associates.
d Frank Lloyd Wright. Solomon R. Guggenheim Museum, New York, 1959.

a

b

Ways to Achieve Unity

Proximity

An easy way to gain unity—to make separate elements look as if they belong together—is by *proximity*, or simply putting these elements close together. The four elements in **a** appear isolated, as floating bits with no relationship to each other. By putting them close together **(b)**, we begin to see them as a total, related pattern. Proximity is a common unifying factor. By it we recognize constellations in the skies and in fact are able to read. Change the proximity scheme that makes letters into words, and reading is impossible.

In El Greco's painting **(c)**, there is a large amount of stormy, though essentially negative, empty space. The smaller nude figures, however, do not float haphazardly in the turbulent background. Instead, they are grouped together, making a horizontal unit across the painting. Arms and legs reach out to touch adjoining figures so that the bodies come together. The drapery on the ground also unites the saint's figure with those behind.

Paul Wonner's painting **(d)** is an interesting collection of still-life objects that are essentially isolated from each other. But notice how the very careful placement and the strategic use of shadows visually tie the elements together by proximity. Our eyes move smoothly from one item to the next.

Proximity *is* the simplest way to achieve unity, and many artworks employ this technique. Without proximity (with largely isolated elements), the artist must put greater stress on the other methods to unify an image.

a If they are isolated from one another, elements appear unrelated.
b Placing elements near each other enables us to see them in a pattern.
c El Greco. *The Vision of St. John.* 1608–14. Oil on canvas, 7'3½" × 6'4" (2.22 × 1.93 m). Metropolitan Museum of Art, New York (Rogers Fund, 1956).
d Paul Wonner. *Dutch Still-Life with Stuffed Birds and Chocolates,* detail. 1981. Acrylic on canvas, 6 × 4' (1.8 × 1.22 m). Collection Harry Cohn, Hillsborough, CA.

d

Unity

Ways to Achieve Unity

Repetition

A most valuable and widely used device for achieving visual unity is *repetition*. As the term implies, something simply repeats in various parts of the design to relate the parts to each other. The element that repeats may be almost anything—a color, a shape, a texture, a direction or angle. In the lithograph by Robert Rauschenberg **(a)**, the repetition is very apparent; indeed, the two outermost forms are almost identical. But all the forms repeat some visual charac-

teristics: the rectangles with a triangular top, the texture of various wrapping papers and tapes, and the bits of type and lettering that reappear. The forms all seem related to each other.

Louise Nevelson's sculpture **(b)** also shows unity by repetition. The complicated pattern of small fragments of wood over the whole surface is a unifying element in itself, almost reminiscent of a Gothic cathedral's intricate facade. But another factor of visual unity is the frequent repetition of vertical rec-

tangular boxes, each one enclosing and framing varying patterns of small details. The repetition of these larger shapes welds the entire pattern into a coherent composition.

Similarly, in naturalistic art with subject matter, repetition can be a unifying factor. In Degas' *The Millinery Shop* **(c)**, notice how often the artist repeats a circle motif—the hats; the flowers and bows; the woman's head, bosom, and skirt. The painting is a whole design of circles broken by a few verticals (the hat stand, the ribbons, the back draperies) and a triangle or so (the table, the woman's bent arm, and the front hat's ribbons). When we look beyond the subject matter in art, we begin to recognize the artist's use of repetition to create a sense of unity.

In paintings or designs with color, this element can be an immediate way to create unity.

a Robert Rauschenberg. *Tampa 2*. 1973. Three-color lithograph and blueprint, 2′5½″ × 6′2½″ (0.75 × 1.89 m). Courtesy Graphic Studio, Art Department, University of South Florida, Tampa.
b Louise Nevelson. *Tide I, Tide*. 1963. Wood, approx. 9 × 12′ (2.74 × 3.66 m). Collection Mr. and Mrs. Albert List, Byram, CT.
c Edgar Degas. *The Millinery Shop*. 1882. Oil on canvas, 39⅛ × 43⅜″ (99 × 110 cm). Art Institute of Chicago (Mr. and Mrs. Lewis L. Coburn Memorial Collection).

a

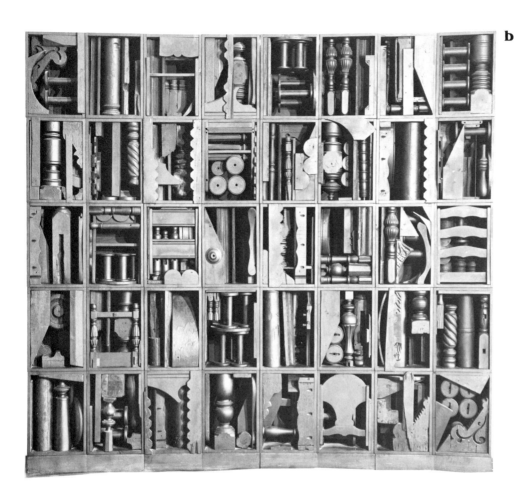

b

c

a

b

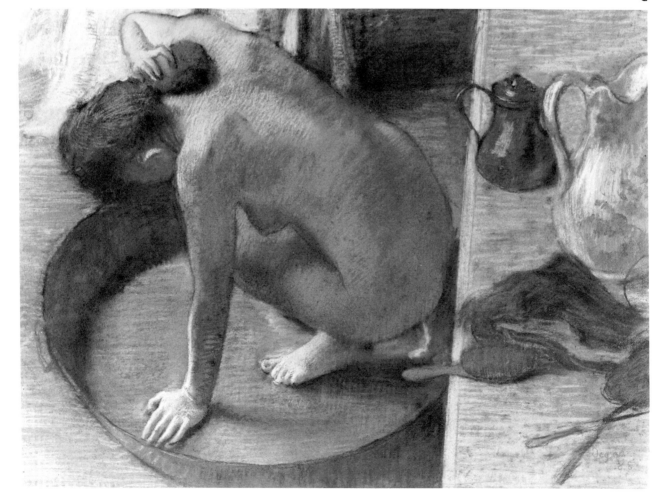

c

Ways to Achieve Unity

Continuation

A third way to achieve unity is by *continuation*, a more subtle device than proximity or repetition, which are fairly obvious. Continuation, naturally, means that something "continues"—usually a line, an edge, or a direction from one form to another. The viewer's eye is carried smoothly from one to the next.

The design in **a** is unified by the closeness and the character of the elements. In **b** though, the shapes seem even more a unit, since they are arranged in such a way that one's vision flows easily from one element to the next. The shapes no longer float casually. They are now organized into a definite, set pattern.

In the pastel drawing by Degas **(c)**, a minute's study reveals many places where the eye is carried from one form to another by placement. The line of the round tub starts at the bather's hairline, meets her fingertips, and joins the vertical line of the shelf where the brush handle overlaps. The circular shape of the bather's hips is tangential to the same shelf edge. Notice the careful arrangement of the objects on the shelf—how each item barely touches or carries the eye to another. That at first glance the arrangement seemed casual and unplanned only adds to our admiration of the artist.

Continuation is the standard device employed by graphic designers planning layouts for books, magazine editorial pages, advertisements, brochures, and so on. In each case the artist must somehow create a sense of visual unity from the very disparate elements of printed headlines, blocks of copy, photographs, and trademarks. Lining up various shapes with a continuation of edges **(d)** is the most practical and satisfactory solution.

Incidentally, if you analyze almost any page in this book, you will have a clear example of the principle of continuation applied to practical design.

---

a Proximity and similarity unify a design.
b The unity of the same design is intensified when the elements are brought into contact with each other in a continuing line.
c Edgar Degas. *The Tub.* 1886. Pastel, 23½ × 32⅓" (60 × 82 cm). Louvre, Paris.
d B. Martin Pedersen. Page Layout: *Leonardo Da Vinci.* U & lc, International Typeface Corp. March 1982.

d

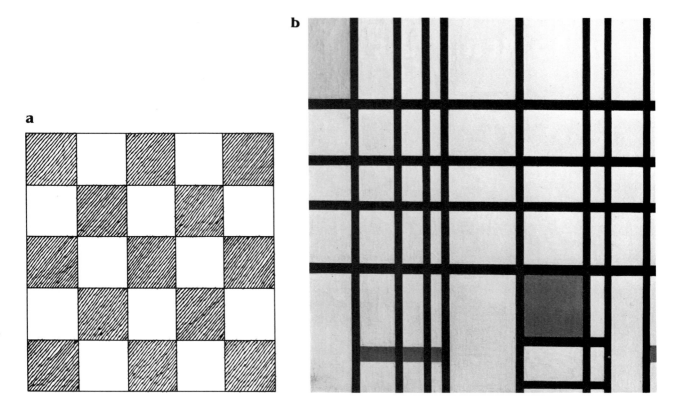

a

c

Unity with Variety

Unity

Design implies unity, a harmonious pattern or order established among the various elements. However, it is possible to make a pattern so highly unified that the result, instead of being visual satisfaction, rather quickly becomes visual boredom. The checkerboard design in **a** is an example. With its scrupulous use of proximity, constant repetition, and careful lining up of the elements, the design is an excellent example of unity—and also quite a dull thing to look at. The designer's aim is to achieve unity, but a unity that branches out into variations that relieve boredom. *Unity with variety* is the oft-quoted artistic ideal, or *theme and variations* as the idea is aptly called in music. Shapes may repeat, but perhaps in different sizes; colors may repeat, but perhaps in different values. The easiest way to explain is to look at examples.

The Mondrian painting **(b)** in many ways resembles the checkerboard, but how much more visually interesting it is. This interest comes basically from an application of the unity-with-variety principle. The varying sizes and shapes of the rectangles, the subtle changes in the thickness of the black lines, the irregular placement of a few colored shapes, the delicate variations of horizontal and vertical emphasis—all these serve to maintain our interest far longer than does the checkerboard design.

Variety is necessary in all types of designs, not only in abstract patterns such as the Mondrian. In Vermeer's painting **(c)**, an almost endless variety of rectangles can be found framing and emphasizing the different-sized and colored circular forms on and around the central subject.

The quilted tapestry **(d)** has a unity based on repetition of triangular shapes. A great deal of variety is introduced: the triangles are different sizes, and the colors and patterns of the many materials vary. Notice how the lines of stitching reinforce the triangle theme and, in effect, create countless other triangles.

---

a Unity without variety can result in a monotonous design.

b Piet Mondrian. *Composition with Red, Yellow, and Blue.* 1937–42. Oil on canvas, 28⅝ × 27¼″ (73 × 69 cm). Tate Gallery, London.

c Jan Vermeer. *The Love Letter.* 1666. Oil on canvas, 17¼ × 15¼″ (44 × 39 cm). Rijksmuseum, Amsterdam.

d Susan Hoffman. *Invention in the Spirit of J. S. Bach.* 1975. Quilted tapestry, 7′9″ × 6′10″ (2.36 × 2.08 m). Courtesy Kornblee Gallery, New York.

d

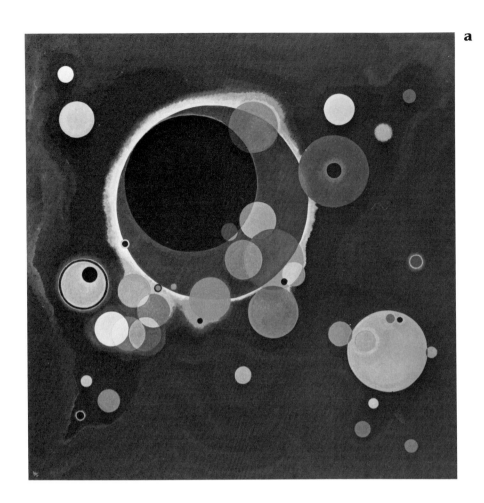

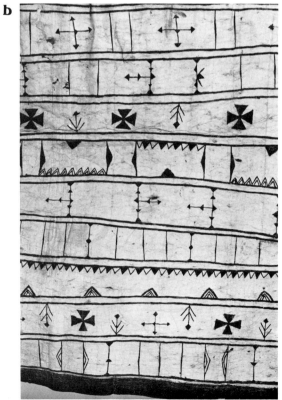

Unity with Variety

Unity

Is the principle of *unity with variety* a conscious, planned ingredient supplied by the artist or designer, or is it something that a confident designer produces automatically? There is no real answer. The only certainty is that the principle can be seen in art from every different period, culture, and geographic area.

Kandinsky's painting **(a)** is titled *Several Circles, No. 323*. The decision to create a composition unified by the repetition of circles was clearly an initial and deliberate choice by the artist. The changes in size and tone of the various circles must also have been purposeful because these changes provide the interest of variety to the painting.

The use of unity with variety displayed by the piece of tapa cloth **(b)** done by a native of Samoa suggests a more intuitive approach. Since many such designs employ tradi-

tional motifs, the method was undoubtedly "learned," but not at an art school or from a textbook. Yet the design illustrates the principle so clearly. Each horizontal band contains similar linear elements, with triangles and arrows repeated over and over. But the sizes vary, and each area combines the elements in a different manner. The idea of related variations seems to provide a basic visual satisfaction that can be arrived at without theoretical discussions of aesthetics.

A conscious use of unity with variety does not necessarily lessen our

pleasure as viewers. A very obvious use of the principle is not a drawback. Little Moreton Hall **(c)** is a visual delight. The complicated structure has been clearly unified by the lively patterns of timber and plaster that cover its exterior. Each part of the building continues the basic black-and-white design of the English Tudor *half-timbered* style. But each wing, often each floor, gives us new patterns, new motifs, and slight but definite variations. This unity didn't just happen; it was certainly carefully planned, and the result is magnificent.

a Wassily Kandinsky. *Several Circles, No. 323*. 1926. Oil on canvas, 4′7⅛″ (1.4 m) square. Solomon R. Guggenheim Museum, New York.
b Tapa cloth, from Samoa. 5′6″ × 3′4″ (1.68 × 1.02 m). American Museum of Natural History, New York.
c Little Moreton Hall, Cheshire, England. c. 1559–89.

c

Unity

Unity with Variety

Emphasis on Unity

In the application of any art principle, wide flexibility is possible within the general framework of the guideline. So it is with the idea of *unity with variety*. To say a design must contain both the ordered quality of unity and the lively quality of variety does not limit or inhibit the artist. The principle can encompass a wide variety of extremely different visual images.

These pages show successful examples where the unifying element of repetition is emphasized. Variety *is* present, but admittedly in a subtle, understated way. The 17th-century portrait **(a)** intrigues us in the same way we are fascinated in life when we meet "identical" twins. Such perfect repetition is unexpected, so we proceed to search for the tiny differences and the variety we know exist in nature and, hence, in art.

The repetition in Warhol's painting **(b)** is constant; there are a hundred repetitions of precisely the same image. But the repetitive, unrelieved quality is the basic point and dictated the design. The painting contains a serious comment on our taken-for-granted daily lives. The design reflects life today, where we are bombarded with insistent and strident repetition of the same commercial images over and over.

The visual unity gained by repetition is immediately apparent, in fact almost overwhelmingly so, in the design of the apartment house in **c**. Buildings like this in the stark, unadorned architecture of the *International Style* have come under severe criticism in recent years. They are often described as "too dull," "cold and sterile," and having "the visual appeal of an ice-cube tray." Many of these comments are by people who have never read or heard of the phrase "unity with variety." Nevertheless, they are using the basic concept in their criticism. What these comments truly mean is that the design has an overwhelming unity, but the variety is so subtle as to be insufficient for the particular viewer's taste. The "correct" balance between unity and variety—between control and spontaneous freedom—varies with the individual artist, with the theme or purpose, and eventually with the viewer.

a British School. *The Cholmondeley Sisters.* c. 1600–10. Oil on wood, 2'11" × 5'8" (0.89 × 1.73 m). Tate Gallery, London.

b Andy Warhol. *100 Soup Cans.* 1962. Oil on canvas, 6' × 4'4" (1.83 × 1.32 m). Albright-Knox Art Gallery, Buffalo, NY. (Gift of Seymour H. Knox, 1963).

c Ludwig Mies van der Rohe. Lake Shore Apartments, Chicago. 1950–52.

a

b

c

Unity

Unity with Variety

Emphasis on Variety

Life is not always orderly and rational. Often life brings surprises, the unexpected, and experiences that seem chaotic and hectic. To express this phase of life, many artists have purposely chosen to underplay the unifying aspects of their work and let the elements appear, at least superficially, uncontrolled and free of any formal design restraints. The examples here show works where the element of *variety* is paramount.

The immediate impression of Richard Hamilton's collage **(a)** is one of a haphazard conglomeration of incongruous images. That, of course, is the point. The collage is as wildly eccentric as the disjointed, fragmented images we see each day (and take for granted) on our television screens and in our newspapers. The many commercial images included mock the importance of such elements in our society. Again, the theme has dictated the design.

The title of Soutine's painting **(b)** tells us it is a picture of a hill. Perhaps there is a suggestion of roofs and trees, but the wild, almost uncontrolled brushstrokes in thick paint create essentially a nonobjective image of pure tone and texture.

The Pollock painting in **c** is similar, but makes no pretense of relating to a natural scene. Twisting linear forms now dominate, but the unplanned, spontaneous feeling pervades the image. Dynamics and change are the subject matter. In galleries or museums, when expressionist abstractions such as **c** are exhibited, one constantly overhears such criticisms as "I don't like it—too messy," "too wild and uncontrolled," and even "My two-year-old could do *that*." What these self-styled critics are saying is that the variety in such a picture is extremely obvious, but their eyes cannot discern any sense of order or unity imposed on that variety. The scales have tipped too far in one direction for them.

Without some aspects of unity, an image becomes chaotic and quickly "unreadable." Without some elements of variety, an image is lifeless and dull and becomes uninteresting. Neither utter confusion nor utter regularity are visually desirable. Beyond this general guideline, the options of the artist are very broad.

a Richard Hamilton. *Just What Is It That Makes Today's Homes So Different, So Appealing?* 1956. Collage on paper, 10⅛ × 9¾" (26 × 25 cm). Kunsthalle, Tübingen, Collection Professor Dr. Georg Zundel, West Germany.

b Chaim Soutine. *Hill at Céret.* c. 1921. Oil on canvas, 29¼ × 21⅝" (74 × 55 cm). Los Angeles County Museum of Art (purchase).

c Jackson Pollock. *One (Number 31, 1950).* 1950. Oil and enamel paint on canvas, 8'10" × 17'5⅝" (2.69 × 5.32 m). Museum of Modern Art, New York (gift of Sidney Janis).

a

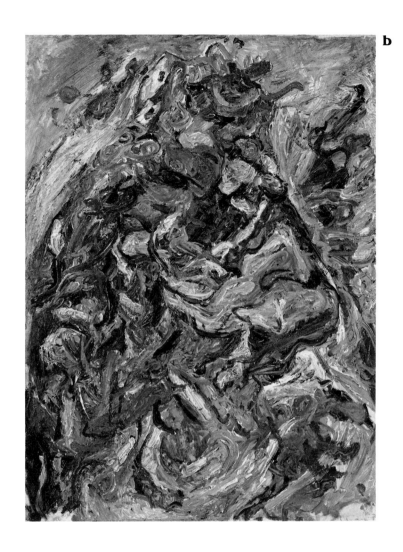

b

c

2

Emphasis/
Focal Point

Emphasis/Focal Point

Introduction

The designer's main enemy is boredom. It is almost better for viewers to stand and revile your image than to pass it quickly with a bored "ho-hum." Your job is to catch attention and provide a pattern that stimulates the viewer by offering some visual satisfaction. Nothing will guarantee success, but one device that can help is a point of emphasis, or *focal point.* This attracts attention and encourages the viewer to look further.

In a picture or design with a theme to relate, the viewer can be shown immediately that "Here is the most important character or element." *Mourning Picture* (a) is a haunting picture done by the American artist Edwin Romanzo Elmer soon after the death of his young daughter. The child dominates the picture and is the first thing we see. She is the largest figure and stands alone on the left side with her head carefully in silhouette against the light sky. The sharp contrast of her dark and light dress with the white lamb also attracts our eye. Other elements call our attention to her, especially the light doll carriage on the lawn. The artist's chosen emphasis is unmistakable.

Even in purely abstract or nonobjective patterns, a focal point will attract the viewer's eye and give some contrast and visual excitement. The slanted V-shape in the center of Kline's painting (b) is a brilliant, light element. This brightness stands out against the dark shapes and immediately establishes the feeling of dynamic movement that permeates the composition.

There can be more than one focal point, but the designer must be careful. Sometimes secondary points of emphasis that have lesser attention value than the focal point are called *accents.* A focal point and several accents can be very effective. On the other hand, several focal points of equal emphasis can turn the design into a three-ring circus where the viewer does not know where to look first. Interest is replaced by confusion: when *everything* is emphasized, *nothing* is emphasized.

a Edwin Romanzo Elmer. *Mourning Picture.* 1890. Oil on canvas, 28 × 36" (71 × 92 cm). Smith College Museum of Art, Northampton, MA (purchase)
b Franz Kline. *King Oliver.* 1958. Oil on canvas, 8'3" × 6'5½" (2.51 × 2.1 m). Collection Mr. and Mrs. Donald Grossman, New York.

a

b

Emphasis/Focal Point

Emphasis by Contrast

Very often in art the pictorial emphasis is clear, and in simple compositions (such as a portrait) the focal point is obvious. But the more complicated the pattern, the more necessary or helpful a focal point may become in organizing the design.

As a general rule, a focal point results when one element differs from the others. Whatever interrupts an overall feeling or pattern automatically attracts the eye by this difference. The possibilities are almost endless:

When most of the elements are vertical, a few horizontal forms break the pattern and become focal points.

When most elements are irregular, spontaneous forms, an almost geometric square shape breaks the pattern and becomes the focal point (**a**).

In a design consisting of large smooth planes, a small, linear, detailed element is emphasized (**b**).

When many elements are about the same size, the one that is much larger is visually important (**c**).

In a design of mainly abstract forms, the occasional recognizable image becomes a focus of attention (**d**).

This list could go on and on; many other possibilities will occur to you. Sometimes this idea is called *emphasis by contrast*. The element that contrasts with, rather than continues, the prevailing design scheme becomes the focal point.

a Sam Francis. *Facing Within*. 1975. Acrylic on canvas, 5'6" × 7' (1.68 × 2.13 m). Collection Byron Meyer, San Francisco, CA.

b Elie Nadelman. *Man in the Open Air*. c. 1915. Bronze, height 4'6½" (1.38 m). Museum of Modern Art, New York (gift of William S. Paley).

c Emperor Otto II, from the *Registrum Gregorii*. Trier, c. 985. Manuscript illumination, 10⅝ × 7⅞" (27 × 20 cm). Musée Condé, Chantilly.

d Ceri Richards. *Major-Minor Orange Blue*. 1970. Screenprint, 29⅞ × 21¾" (76 × 55 cm).

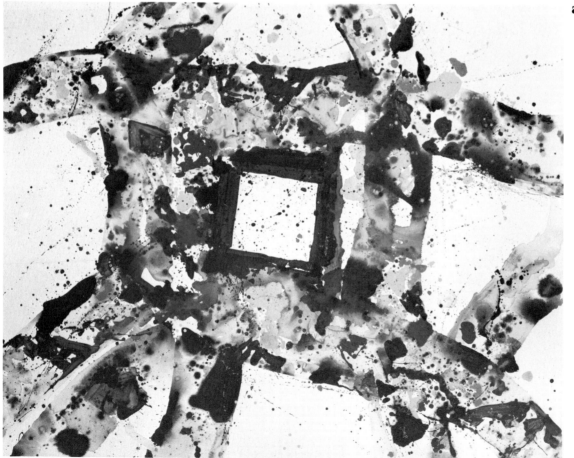

a

b

c

d

Emphasis/Focal Point

Emphasis by Isolation

A variation on the device of emphasis by contrast is the useful technique of *emphasis by isolation.* When one item is isolated or sits apart from the other elements or groups of elements, it becomes a focal point. Just by its separation, an element takes on visual importance. This is contrast, of course, but it is contrast of placement, not form. In such a case, the element need not be any different from the others. The black square in **a** is like others in the design; but its placement away from them draws the eye, and it becomes the focal point.

In the still life by Cézanne **(b)** the pitcher at left repeats the color of the bowl and the cloth, and the design on it repeats the fruit forms. In short, the pitcher is part of a unified composition, but it gains visual importance because it sits away from the items grouped together at right. The pitcher is an emphasized element only through its detached position.

John Trumbull leaves no room for doubt about the point of emphasis in painting **c**. We cannot miss the generals isolated in the middle, with Washington silhouetted against the sky.

Putting the focal point directly in the center does look slightly contrived. However, it is wise to remember that a focal point placed too close to an edge will have a tendency to pull the viewer's eye right out of the picture. Notice in the Cézanne still life **(b)** how the verticals of the drapery on the left side keep the isolated pitcher from directing our gaze out of the picture.

a Isolating an element draws our attention to it.
b Paul Cézanne. *Still Life with Apples and Peaches.* c. 1905. Oil on canvas, 32 × 39⅝" (81 × 100 cm). National Gallery of Art, Washington, DC (gift of Eugene and Agnes Meyer, 1959).
c John Trumbull. *The Surrender of Lord Cornwallis.* 1787–94. Oil on canvas, 20⅞ × 30⅝" (53 × 78 cm). Copyright Yale University Art Gallery, New Haven, CT.

a

b

c

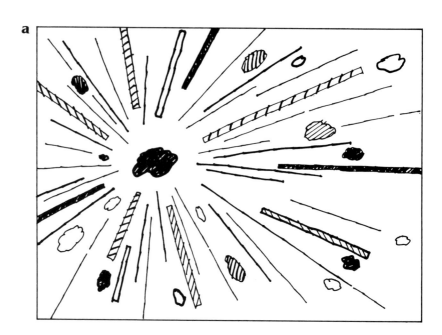

Emphasis by Placement

Emphasis/Focal Point

The placement of elements in a design may function in another way to create emphasis. If many elements point to one item, our attention is directed there, and a focal point results. A radial design is a perfect example of this device. Just as all forms radiate from the convergent focus, so they also repeatedly lead our eyes back to this central element. As **a** illustrates, this central element may be like other forms in the design; the emphasis results from the placement, not from any difference in character, of the form itself.

Radial designs are more common in architecture than in two-dimensional art. The more subtle variation in painting occurs when many figures *look* (or sometimes point) in a common direction. In life when we see someone staring or pointing a certain way, we have an almost uncontrollable urge to look there. This happens in art, too. In Curry's scene of a fundamentalist baptism by immersion **(b)**, all the figures look directly at the preacher and the girl, automatically directing our eyes there as well. Even the lines of the windmill and the roofs of the barn and house direct our eyes to the focal point of these two figures.

In the photograph shown in **c**, the placement is important for emphasis. The police officer, being the only figure, is a natural focal point. Beyond this, his placement at the point where other background lines converge (especially the perspective diagonals of the brick wall) reinforces his dramatic emphasis.

The effect need not be as obvious as in these examples. However, once your focal point has been decided upon, it is wise to avoid having other major or visually important elements point or lead the eye *away* from it. Confusion of emphasis can result.

---

a Our eyes are drawn to the central element of this design by all the elements radiating from it.
b John Steuart Curry. *Baptism in Kansas.* 1928. Oil on canvas, 3'4" × 4'2" (1.02 × 1.27 m). Whitney Museum of American Art, New York.
c Bill Brandt, *Policeman in Bermonday.* N.d. Photograph.

c

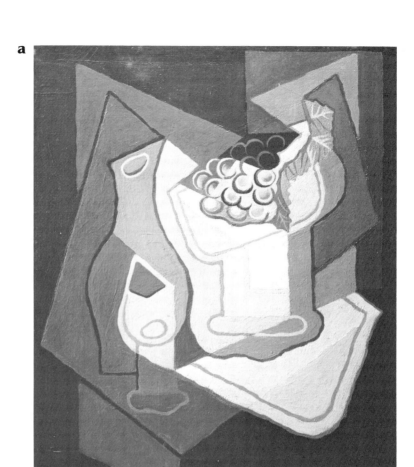

a

b

Degree of Emphasis

In discussing the creation and use of a focal point, a word of warning is in order. There is no real difficulty in introducing a new contrasting element into a design. However, any emphasis must be created with some subtlety and sense of restraint. The focal point must remain a part of the overall design, rather than become an alien element that looks totally out of place. Imagine a design of soft grayish-blue squares with one enormous brilliant orange circle. The focal point is obvious, *so* obvious it may overwhelm the rest of the design completely. The viewer's eye certainly sees the focal point, but because this point has overpowering dominance, the eye never leaves it to see the rest of the design.

In Juan Gris' still life **(a)**, the massed group of linear circles defining the bunch of grapes is a focal point. But the values of this element are repeated in several other places.

And circular forms are seen elsewhere, with the bottle top and glass bottom repeating the same small linear circle motif. The focal point established is not a completely unrelated element.

In **b** the center church steeple in the distance is a clear focal point. However, it remains a part of the total pattern. The steeple's tonal values are close to those of the sky, so it visually stays back. Its large vertical mass contrasts with the horizontals implied in the foreground foliage and the sky. But vertical movement is repeated in other forms on the left and right. Most importantly, the steeple is painted in the same small, broken brushstrokes that are used to

define all the other forms and the background sky. The emphasis is clear, yet a totally unified element with the rest of the painting. See the difference in **c**, where the isolated black shape is very different from any of the subtle semicircular elements at the right. It *is* a focal point, but seems too dominant and unconnected to the rest of the pattern.

A specific theme may, at times, call for a very dominant, even overwhelming, focal point. But, in general, the principle of unity and the creation of a harmonious pattern with related elements is more important than the injection of a focal point if this point would jeopardize the design's unity.

---

a Juan Gris. *Bottle, Glass and Fruit Dish*. 1921. Oil on canvas, 24 × 20″ (61 × 50 cm). Oeffentliche Kunstsammlung Basel, Basel.
b Christian Rohlfs. *St. Patroclus in Soest*. 1905–06. Oil on cardboard, 26¾ × 38⅝″ (68 × 98 cm). Wallraf- Richartz Museum, Cologne.
c Too much emphasis detracts from the unity of a design.

c

Absence of Focal Point

A definite focal point is not a necessity in creating a successful design. It is a tool that artists may or may not use, depending on their aims. Many paintings have an ambiguous emphasis, and different viewers will see different elements as the most important. Indeed, many artists have purposely ignored the whole idea of a focal point. Irene Rice Pereira's painting (**a**) is an example. Similar geometric forms extend over the whole painting. The artist creates an interesting feeling of depth and light which is puzzling and ambiguous. But no one area stands out; the painting has no real starting point or visual climax.

Some art forms, by their very nature, rule out the use of a focal point. Woven and printed fabrics (**b**) generally have no focal point, but consist of an unstressed repetition of a motif over the whole surface. A focal point on draperies, bedspreads, or upholstery might be distracting. In clothing, the focal point is provided by the design of the garment.

Since a focal point is such a common artistic device, sometimes attention can be gotten by simply *not* using one. The poster advertisement in **c** appears at first glance to be a totally repetitive pattern, but we find ourselves searching out subtle differences in each of the similar pictures. The designer has achieved his goal: Our eye is attracted by the unusual overall emphasis of the layout, and time is spent studying the image.

a Irene Rice Pereira. *Green Depth.* 1944. Oil on canvas, 31 × 42″ (79 × 107 cm). Metropolitan Museum of Art, New York (George A. Hearn Fund, 1944).
b Tricia Guild. *Fossils.* Printed cotton. Courtesy Brunschwig & Fils, Inc., New York.
c Robert Weaver. *To Be Good Is Not Enough, When You Dream of Being Great.* Poster advertising classes at the School of Visual Arts, New York.

c

3

Balance

Balance

Example **a** is a cropped detail showing only a part of a portrait by Thomas Eakins. The entire painting is shown in **b**. Why do we find **b** a more satisfactory image than **a**? Partially, of course, because we like to see more of the subject; cutting through the woman's face seems curious. But the main reason for our preference concerns the principle of *balance*. Without seeing the chair and the position of the woman within the surrounding space **a** puts all the visual weight on the left side. There is nothing on the right side to compensate and provide any sort of equilibrium. The detail is off-balance. The total painting shows a much more equal distribution of weight.

A sense of balance is innate; as children we develop a sense of balance in our bodies and observe balance in the world around us. Lack of balance, or *imbalance*, disturbs us.

We carefully avoid dangerously leaning trees, rocks, furniture, and ladders. But even where no physical danger is present, as in a design or painting, we still feel more comfortable with a balanced pattern (**c**).

In assessing pictorial balance, we always assume a center vertical axis and usually expect to see some kind of equal weight (visual weight) distribution on either side. This axis functions as the fulcrum on a scale or see-saw, and the two sides should achieve a sense of equilibrium. When this equilibrium is not present, as in **d**, a certain vague uneasiness or dissatisfaction results. We feel a need to rearrange the elements, in the same way that we automatically straighten a tilted picture on the wall.

---

a Thomas Eakins. *Miss Van Buren,* detail of **b**.
b Thomas Eakins. *Miss Van Buren.* c. 1886–90. Oil on canvas, 44½ × 32" (113 × 81 cm). Phillips Collection, Washington, DC.
c Paolo Veronese. *Christ in the House of Levi.* 1573. Oil on canvas, 18'2" × 42' (5.54 × 12.8 m). Accademia, Venice.
d An unbalanced design leaves the viewer with a vague uneasiness.

a

b

d

Balance

Introduction

Balance—some equal distribution of visual weight—is a universal aim of composition. The vast majority of pictures we see have been consciously balanced by the artist. However, this does not mean there is no place in art for purposeful imbalance. An artist may, because of a particular theme or topic, expressly desire that a picture raise uneasy, disquieting responses in the viewer.

In this instance, imbalance can be a useful tool. Even without such a motive, an occasional almost imbalanced image, such as that in the Japanese screen **(a)**, intrigues us and attracts our attention for exactly this unexpected quality.

In speaking of pictorial balance, we are almost always referring to horizontal balance, the right and left sides of the image. Artists consider vertical balance as well, with a horizontal axis dividing top and bottom. Again a certain general equilibrium is usually desirable. However, because of our sense of gravity, we are accustomed to seeing more weight toward the bottom, with a resulting stability and calm **(b)**. The farther up in the format the main distribution of weight or visual interest occurs, the more unstable and dynamic the image becomes. In Paul Klee's whimsical *Tightrope Walker* **(c)**, the instability of the image expresses the theme perfectly. The linear patterns build up vertically until we reach the teetering figure near the top. The artist can manipulate the vertical balance freely to fit a particular theme or purpose.

a Hōitsu Kishin. *Persimmons.* c. 1816. Screen, two-fold pair. Ink and color on paper, 5′5¼″ × 5′4″ (1.66 × 1.63 m). Metropolitan Museum of Art, New York (Rogers Fund, 1957).
b Dean Fausett. *Derby View.* 1939. Oil tempera on canvas, 24⅛ × 40″ (61 × 102 cm). Museum of Modern Art, New York (purchased from the Southern Vermont Artists' Exhibition at Manchester with a fund given anonymously).
c Paul Klee. *Tightrope Walker.* 1923. Color lithograph, 17⅛ × 10⅝″ (44 × 26 cm). Museum of Modern Art, New York (given anonymously).

a

b

c

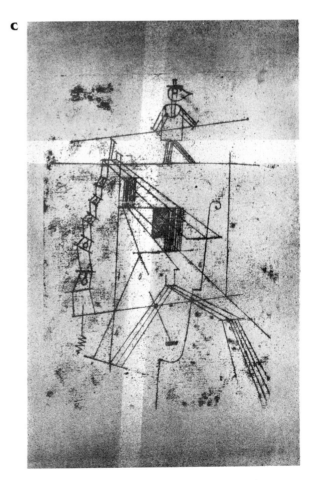

a

b

Symmetrical Balance

Balance

The simplest type of balance—to create and to recognize—is called *symmetrical* balance. In symmetrical balance, like shapes are repeated in the same positions on either side of a central vertical axis **(a)**. One side, in effect, becomes the mirror image of the other side. Symmetrical balance has a seemingly basic appeal for us. Children and beginning art students will almost instinctively create patterns with symmetrical balance. Psychologists ascribe this to our awareness of the fact that our bodies are basically symmetrical, so that we intuitively extend the principle to our first artistic efforts.

Conscious symmetrical repetition, while clearly creating perfect balance, can be undeniably static, so that the term *formal* balance is used to describe the same idea. There is nothing wrong with quiet formality. In fact, this characteristic is often desired in some art, notably in architecture. The Colonial house in **b** has a rigidly repetitive pattern, which results in a dignified, calm, sedate facade—qualities many people like in a home. We like a house to look stable, to be a quiet refuge from the world's daily problems. This accounts for the continued popularity of symmetrical designs in many styles of domestic architecture.

Government buildings, such as statehouses, city halls, palaces, and courthouses, often exploit the properties of symmetrical balance.

A feeling of permanence and imposing formality is important in such public statements of power. Numerous examples are to be found throughout the world.

Symmetrical balance does not, by itself, preordain any specific visual result. Examples **b** and **c** are both symmetrical facades, yet they create very different impressions. The ordered, dignified austerity of the Colonial house **(b)** is certainly not present in the Spanish cathedral **(c)**. The latter is a busy, excitingly ornate building with only the symmetrical organization molding the masses of niches, balustrades, columns, and statuary into a unified and coherent visual pattern.

a In symmetrical balance, one side of a design mirrors the other.
b Vassal (Longfellow) House, Cambridge, MA. 1750.
c José Peña and Fernando de Casas. Cathedral, Santiago de Compostela, Spain. 1667–1750.

c

a

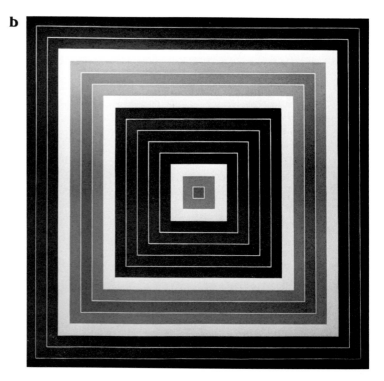

b

Symmetrical Balance

Balance

Symmetrical balance is rarer in painting than in architecture. However, in certain instances it has proved to be a useful compositional device.

Sometimes the subject matter makes symmetrical balance appropriate. A dignified, solemn subject such as the Madonna enthroned **(a)** clearly calls for the qualities symmetrical balance can impart. In this example, the Madonna is presented in stately, regal splendor. Her position on the central axis gives her primary emphasis. You will notice that in painting, elements or figures may vary slightly on the opposing sides without changing the basic effect of symmetry. Many religious paintings that were intended as altarpieces in churches employed symmetry so as not to interrupt the prevailing tenor of the architectural setting.

Contemporary Color Field painting often uses symmetrical balance for a different, very specific reason. This style is sometimes referred to as Minimal Art, since the artists who practice it seek to reduce art to a minimum of aesthetic considerations. Example **b**, a painting by Frank Stella, can show the concept. To focus our attention on color relationships, Stella severely plays down all the other elements. Subject matter is ignored, and the repetitive composition of squares provides no contrast of shape. The symmetrical, formal positioning can be understood quickly and would not intrigue the viewer. Thus, one's whole attention is directed to the tone differences. Such paintings make full use of symmetrical balance's only negative aspect—its regularity of repetition and lack of variety.

Quiet formality is certainly not a characteristic of **c**. A painting based on the innumerable rock posters from the psychedelic, drug-oriented culture of the 1960s is perhaps the last place we would expect to find symmetrical balance. But it illustrates another use of symmetry. If the artist's design involves a great number of figures or elements, then symmetrical balance (which in other cases appears a rather contrived device) can organize a possible confusion into a readable pattern. In this painting **(c)** only the symmetrical repetition keeps a fantastically complicated design of "jumpy" shapes organized and at least somewhat coherent. Thus, the simplicity of symmetrical balance can be an asset if the design elements are busy and complex.

a Giovanni Bellini. *Madonna and Child Enthroned* (San Giobbe Altarpiece). c. 1485. Panel, 15′4″ × 8′4″ (4.67 × 2.54 m). Accademia, Venice.

b Frank Stella. *Gran Cairo.* 1962. Synthetic polymer on canvas, 7′1½″ (2.17 m) square. Whitney Museum of American Art, New York (gift of the Friends of the Whitney Museum of American Art).

c Karl Wirsum. *Screamin' J. Hawkins.* 1968. Acrylic on canvas, 47½ × 37″ (122 × 91 cm). Art Institute of Chicago (Mr. & Mrs. Frank G. Logan Prize Fund).

c

Balance

Asymmetrical Balance

Introduction

The second type of balance is called *asymmetrical* balance. In this case, balance is achieved with *dissimilar* objects that have equal visual weight or equal eye attraction. Remember the children's riddle: "Which weighs more, a pound of feathers or a pound of lead?" Of course, they both weigh a pound, but the amount and mass of each vary radically. This, then, is the essence of asymmetrical balance.

In the Japanese print (**a**), the mountain is not centered to divide the picture symmetrically. The large mass of the mountain sits to the right of the center axis. But the composition is not off-balance. The left side provides enough visual interest to balance the weight of the large triangular mountain that draws our first attention. This visual interest is provided by the complicated pattern of light clouds against the darker sky, and the dark mass of small triangles, which suggests a forest of trees. The two sides of the composition are thus very different, with dissimilar elements, yet a sense of balance is maintained.

The imposing Ford Foundation Building in **b** is an example of asymmetrical balance in architecture. The weight and eye attraction of the two sides are balanced with very different elements and materials. The strong simple rectangular areas of brown granite on the left are visually balanced by the lighter but more intricate window pattern of reflecting glass on the right. This change and contrast provide visual interest and excitement.

In contrast to symmetrical balance, the effect of asymmetrical balance is more casual, hence the alternate title *informal* balance is often used. The effect is less formal, less contrived in feeling. Symmetry often appears artificial, as our visual experiences in life are rarely symmetrically arranged. Some buildings and interiors are so designed, but even here unless we stand quietly at dead center, our views are always asymmetrical. Asymmetry appears casual and less planned, although obviously this characteristic is misleading. Asymmetrical balance is actually more intricate and complicated to use than symmetrical balance. Merely repeating similar elements in a mirror image on either side of the center is not a difficult design task. But attempting to balance *dissimilar* items involves more complex considerations and more subtle factors.

a Katsushika Hokusai. *South Wind and Clearing Weather,* from *Thirty-Six Views of Fuji.* c. 1820–30. Color woodcut, 10 × 15″ (25 × 38 cm). Metropolitan Museum of Art, New York (Rogers Fund, 1936).
b Kevin Roche, John Dinkeloo and Associates. Ford Foundation Building, New York. 1968.

a

b

a

Asymmetrical Balance

Balance by Color

Studies have proven that our eyes are attracted to color. Given a choice, we will always look at a colored image rather than at one in black and white. Color, therefore, can become a balancing factor. A small area of bright color can balance a much larger area of a duller, more neutral color. Our eyes, drawn by the color, see the smaller element to be as interesting and as "heavy" visually as the larger element.

This technique of achieving balance is common in painting. In the work by Gauguin (**a**) the figure at left is wearing a brilliant red-patterned sarong, the figure at right a muumuu of quite neutral, grayish-pink. The areas of color are very different in size, but the artist establishes an equilibrium based on color. Reversing these colors would result in a visual imbalance. The right figure, if dressed in bright, eye-attracting red, would become far too dominant.

In **b** we have a very subtle balance by color. This Japanese print is quite neutral in color; white and warm grays dominate the snow scene. The group of houses sits slightly to the right of the center axis, and the hill fills the left side. On the left is a small figure colored in dull orange, which is a strong color in this context, though it repeats the browns of the houses. This color note is balanced by the much larger area of the sea, which is a cooler tone of blue, repeated in a more neutral, darkening sky above. The essentially "empty" right side has been balanced by color.

Balance by color is a valuable tool allowing a great difference of shapes on either side of the center axis and still achieving equal eye attraction.

---

a Paul Gauguin. *Two Women on a Beach.* 1891. Oil on canvas, 27 × 35½″ (69 × 90 cm). Louvre, Paris.
b Kuniyoshi. *Nichiren in Exile.* c. 1831. Color woodcut, 8¾ × 13½″ (22 × 34 cm). Philadelphia Museum of Art (given by Mrs. John D. Rockefeller).

b

Asymmetrical Balance

Balance by Value

Asymmetrical balance is based on equal eye attraction—dissimilar objects are equally interesting to the eye. One element that attracts our attention is *value* difference, a contrast of light and dark. Example **a** illustrates that black against white gives a stronger contrast than gray against white; therefore, a smaller amount of black is needed to visually balance a larger amount of gray.

An application of this idea in an admittedly not-so-subtle manner is Zurbarán's painting (**b**). The martyred St. Serapion, rather than being centered on the canvas, is mainly on the left side. The saint's head, where our attention naturally goes, is to the left of the center axis. This emphasis is balanced on the right by the greater dark and light contrast in his robes, and also by the piece of paper tacked to the wall—a small white shape that contrasts strongly with the very dark background. Without this tiny element, our attention would focus too strongly on the left side.

The painting by John Singer Sargent (**c**) illustrates the same idea in a less obvious manner. The background room with the figure on the right attracts our attention. This is balanced by the large, rather indistinct, black piano on the left. But the open white pages of music in sharp value contrast with the dark piano provide the actual element of asymmetrical balance. The light curtain and area of light in the lower left provide a further lesser value contrast for balance.

In **d** the strong look of the figure gives emphasis and importance to the left side. The contrast of the white table against the dark background balances the right side.

a A darker, smaller element is visually equal to a lighter, larger one.
b Francisco de Zurbarán. *St. Serapion.* 1628. Oil on canvas, 47½ × 40¾" (121 × 104 cm). Wadsworth Atheneum, Hartford, CT (Ella Gallup Sumner and Mary Catlin Sumner Collection).
c John Singer Sargent. *Le Piano Noir.* 1880. Oil on canvas, 12 × 16" (30 × 41 cm). Private collection.
d George Grosz. *The Engineer Heartfield.* 1920. Photomontage and watercolor, 16½ × 12" (42 × 30 cm). Museum of Modern Art, New York (gift of A. Conger Goodyear).

d

Balance

Asymmetrical Balance

Balance by Shape

The diagram in **a** illustrates balance by shape. Here the two elements are exactly the same color, exactly the same value and texture. The only difference is their shape. The smaller form attracts the eye because of its more complicated contours. Though small, it is as interesting as the much larger, but duller, rectangle.

This type of balance appears in Goya's painting *The Parasol* (**b**). The standing figure is on the central axis, with the woman seated slightly to the left. On the left also the quite large shape of the parasol is defined against a simple dark area of shadowed wall. Clearly, something is needed on the right for balance, and Goya chose the tree that leans to the right. This tree, while slender and delicate, has an intricate pattern of branches and leaves to balance the very simple, elliptical shape of the parasol. In the background, the small shapes of tree foliage are as interesting as the large, dark, somewhat geometric, triangular shadow at left. To put it briefly, the left side consists of large simple shapes, while the right side is composed of smaller, more complicated areas. Together they achieve balance.

The balance of elements in painting **c**, by Sylvia Gosse, shows the same idea. The focal point is the figure on the left, whose large, essentially simple shape is balanced by the pattern of the many complicated mechanical forms of the printing press on the right.

---

a A small, complicated shape is balanced by a larger, more stable shape.

b Francisco Goya. *The Parasol,* cartoon for tapestry. 1777. Oil on canvas, c. 3′5″ × 4′11″ (1.04 × 1.5 m). Prado, Madrid.

c Sylvia Gosse. *The Printer.* 1915–16. Oil on canvas, 40 × 30″ (102 × 76 cm). Borough of Thamesdown–Swindon Permanent Art Collection, Swindon, Wiltshire.

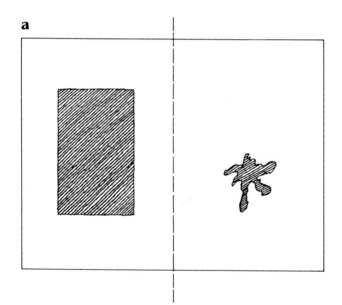

a

b

c

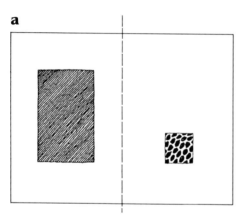

a

b

c

Asymmetrical Balance

Balance

Balance by Texture

Any visual (or photographic) texture with a variegated dark and light pattern holds more interest for the eye than does a smooth, unrelieved surface. The drawing in **a** presents this idea: the smaller, rough-textured area balances the larger, basically untextured area (smoothness is, in a sense, a "texture").

The subject of Vermeer's *Woman with a Lute* (**b**) sits slightly to the left of the center axis and *looks* to the left, further emphasizing that side of the painting. The major balancing element on the right is, of course, the large map on the wall. Important to this composition is the rather busy, detailed texture of light and dark variations; a plain, flat brown area would not have the necessary interest. The shiny nail heads on the dark chair contribute a further balancing interest.

The shiny, reflective surfaces of a silver tea set are the major element in balancing the figures in a painting by Mary Cassatt (**c**). In addition, the fireplace and over-the-mantel elements provide textural interest missing in the uniform pattern of the wallpaper to the left. The advantage of textural balance is the subtlety and the casual, apparently unplanned feeling of the finished image. This apparent informality seems natural and more life-like than would the more formal methods of balance.

Printed text consisting of letters and words in effect creates a visual texture. This is information in symbols that we can read, but the *visual* effect is nothing more than a gray-patterned shape. Depending on the typeface and the layout, this gray area varies in darkness, density, and character, but it is visually textured. The Olivetti advertisement in **d** illustrates this point. Here the small paragraph of text creates a textured area that visually balances the larger shape of the sickle.

---

a A small, textured shape can balance a larger, untextured one.

b Jan Vermeer. *Woman with a Lute*. 1663–64. Oil on canvas, 20¼ × 18" (51 × 46 cm). Metropolitan Museum of Art, New York (bequest of Collis P. Huntington, 1900).

c Mary Cassatt. *A Cup of Tea*. c. 1880. Oil on canvas, 25½ × 36½" (65 × 93 cm). Museum of Fine Arts, Boston (Maria Hopkins Fund).

d Two-page layout from *Early American Tools* (Olivetti Corporation of America). Irwin Glusker, art director and designer; Hans Namuth, photographer.

---

d

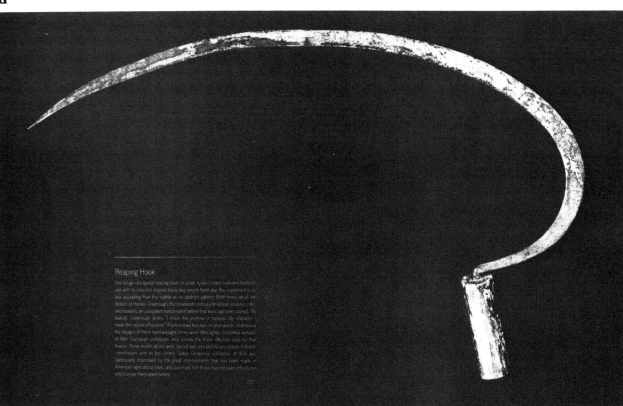

Reaping Hook

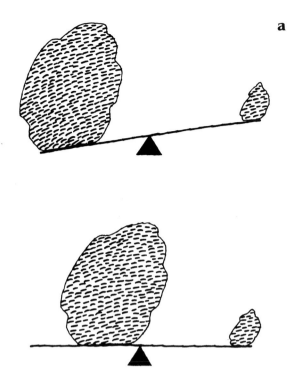

a

b

c

Asymmetrical Balance

Balance by Position

The two see-saw diagrams in **a** illustrate the idea of balance by position. A well-known principle in physics is that two items of unequal weight can be brought to equilibrium by moving the heavier inward toward the fulcrum. In design this means that a large item placed closer to the center can be balanced by a smaller item placed out toward the edge.

Balance by position often lends an unusual, unexpected quality to the composition. The effect not only seems casual and unplanned but also can, at first glance, seem to be in imbalance. A painting by Degas **(b)** shows this quality. With the two dancers mainly to the right of center, the only balancing element on the left is the small gray watering can.

However, its placement, isolated at the left edge of the painting, visually balances the much larger figures.

An unusual painting by Gainsborough **(c)** has obvious emphasis on the left, where the two figures are posed before a large tree. The three detailed trees and the wheat sheaves are smaller elements, but their placement at far right, running off the edge of the picture, provides a very subtle balance.

The same principle is used in **d**, a still life of simplified, abstracted forms. Larger objects are grouped on the left. The neck of the guitar creates a strong horizontal line that leads our eyes to the right. On the right edge of the painting, the smaller, isolated bottle balances the heavier objects on the other side. It is often interesting to mentally move elements in paintings and see how the balance is affected.

---

a A large shape placed near the middle of a design can be balanced by a smaller shape placed toward the outer edge.

b Edgar Degas. *Dancers Practicing at the Bar.* 1877. Oil colors freely mixed with turpentine on canvas, 29¾ × 32″ (76 × 81 cm). Metropolitan Museum of Art, New York (bequest of Mrs. H. O. Havemeyer, 1929, the H. O. Havemeyer Collection).

c Thomas Gainsborough. *Mr. and Mrs. Robert Andrews.* c. 1748–50. Oil on canvas, 27 × 47″ (69 × 119 cm). National Gallery, London (reproduced by courtesy of the Trustees).

d Le Corbusier. *Still Life.* 1920. Oil on canvas, 31⅞ × 39¼″ (81 × 100 cm). Museum of Modern Art, New York (Van Gogh Purchase Fund).

d

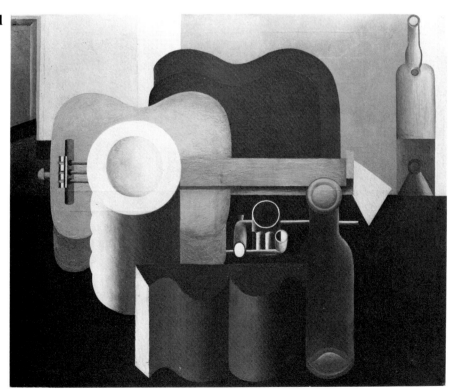

Asymmetrical Balance

Balance by Eye Direction

One further element in achieving asymmetrical balance should be noted. In **a** the many heavier elements on the right all direct our attention automatically to the left, thus building up the smallest of elements into a balancing importance. Asymmetrical balance is based on equal eye attraction, and here the large elements themselves make the small element the focal point.

In Seurat's painting **(b)** the small white gaslight form at left assumes great visual importance from the number of elements that lead our eyes to that side. All the dancers face and kick their legs in this direction, and the dark, diagonal, linear shape of the bass fiddle takes the eye right to this light shape. Almost everywhere we look something works to move our eyes back to the one seemingly unimportant form that balances the whole picture.

The same technique applies in the Art Deco railway poster **(c)**. The large dark locomotive is positioned on the left, but the accentuated perspective lines of the receding train and platform make a sharp arrow that directs attention to the right. Actually, only the few lines of the distant station are on the right side of the design, but the eye direction creates the optical balance.

In this method of balance, the direction in which figures look also applies because we viewers will involuntarily look the same say. Figure **d** illustrates the idea. The soldier's backward glance balances the leftward movement and interest of the horse's head and prancing leg at the left side of the painting. We follow the soldier's look, and this balances the painting.

While not usually the *only* technique of balance employed, the useful device of eye direction is a common practice among artists. Eye direction is carefully plotted by the artist, not only for balance but also for general compositional unity.

a A single small element can be as important as many larger ones if it is made the focal point of the design.

b Georges Seurat. *Le Chahut.* 1890. Oil on canvas, 5′7″ × 4′7″ (1.69 × 1.39 m). Rijksmuseum Kröller-Müller, Otterlo, Netherlands.

c Pierre Fix-Masseau. *Exactitude.* Gouache, after a poster of 1929. 39⅜ × 24½″ (100 × 62 cm). Metropolitan Museum of Art, New York (gift of the Publisher's Office, 1983).

d Théodore Géricault. *Wounded Cuirassier Leaving the Field.* 1814. Oil on canvas, 9′7″ × 7′5⅜″ (2.95 × 2.27 m). Louvre, Paris.

a

b

EXACTITUDE

ETAT

c

d

Asymmetrical Balance

Balance

Analysis Summary

In looking at paintings, you will realize that isolating one technique of asymmetrical balance as we have done is a bit misleading, since the vast majority of works employ several of the methods simultaneously. For the sake of clarity these methods are discussed separately, but the principles often overlap and are often used together. Let us look at just a few examples that make use of several of the factors involved in asymmetrical balance.

The multiple portrait *The Daughters of Edward Darley Boit* (**a**), by Sargent, has an interesting composition with fairly isolated figures and a great amount of dark negative space. The initial emphasis is at the left, where the large vase and almost all the figures are posed. Only the little girl seated on the rug is very slightly to the right of center. The right side of the composition is basically empty space, but a few visually important elements balance the painting. A window in the rear room provides two light areas in high contrast with the darkness. The glimpse of red

curtain at right introduces the brightest color note in the whole painting. The rug provides textural interest. And, finally, the light shape of the second large vase draws our eyes to the very edge of the painting, offsetting the figures clustered near the center.

Painting **b**, by the American artist Richard Diebenkorn, appears at first glance to be an example of imbalance. Certainly, there is a great deal of weight on the left side, where both figures are placed as well as the background windows. In addition, the woman's detailed striped skirt attracts attention in a work where most of the areas are large, flat, abstracted forms. The obvious balancing element is the diagonal stripe on the floor, which forms an "arrow" directing our eye to the right. This

strong light shape against the dark floor immediately attracts our attention. Dark and light contrast also emphasizes the right doorway. Repeating the vertical shape of the figures in a painting filled with horizontal emphasis, the doorway also sits at the very edge of the canvas, thus balancing by position. Finally, through the open door numerous small shapes suggesting the distant landscape are seen. These small forms provide a visual interest lacking in the totally blank white windows on the left. The painting, therefore, uses several devices to establish a subtle sense of balance, while retaining the immediate effect of spontaneous informality.

Notice how shape, value, position, and eye direction are all involved in balancing the Japanese print in **c**.

a John Singer Sargent. *The Daughters of Edward Darley Boit.* 1882. Oil on canvas, 7'3" (2.21 m) square. Museum of Fine Arts, Boston (gift of Mary Louisa Boit, Florence D. Boit, Jane Hubbard Boit, and Julia Overing Boit in memory of their father).
b Richard Diebenkorn. *Man and Woman in Large Room.* 1957. Oil on canvas, 5'11" × 5'3" (1.8 × 1.6 m). Hirshhorn Museum and Sculpture Garden, Smithsonian Institution, Washington, DC.
c Suzuki Harunobu. *Girl with Lantern on Balcony at Night.* c. 1768. Color woodcut, 12¾ × 8¼" (32 × 21 cm). Metropolitan Museum of Art, New York (Fletcher Fund, 1929).

c

Balance

Radial Balance

A third variety of balance is called *radial* balance. Here all the elements radiate or circle out from a common central point. The sun with its emanating rays **(a)** is a familiar symbol that expresses the basic idea. Radial balance is not entirely distinct from symmetrical or asymmetrical balance. It is merely a refinement of one or the other, depending on whether the focus occurs in the middle or off-center.

Circular forms abound in craft areas such as ceramics, where the round shapes of dishes and bowls often make radial balance a natural choice in decorating such objects.

Radial balance also appears in jewelry design. The brooch in **b** is reminiscent of the radial patterns found in snowflakes. Notice how each of the small outer elements makes a radial design in itself. Radial balance has been used frequently in architecture. The round form of domed buildings such as the Roman Pantheon or our nation's Capitol will almost automatically give a radial feeling to the interior.

The major compositional advantage in radial balance is the immediate and obvious creation of a focal point. Perhaps, this is also the reason that such balance seldom occurs

in painting. It might seem a little too contrived and unnatural, a little too obvious to be entirely satisfactory. There can be no doubt that when radial balance *is* used in painting, it is employed in a rather understated manner. Utrillo's Parisian street scene **(c)** has a quite clear radial feeling. The one-point perspective of the receding curbs and rooflines directs the eye to the white cathedral in the distance.

Less obvious, but still with a definite radial feeling, is Bouts' *Last Supper Altarpiece* **(d)**. The positioning of the disciples around the table, all turned and looking inward, creates the radial effect. We can see that the plate in the center of the table is more of a focal point than the figure of Christ, which becomes another of the radiating elements.

The fact that radial balance is rare in formal narrative painting should not deter you from experimenting with it. It can be a useful tool in organization, and some extremely effective designs may result.

a Jean Lurçat. *Soleil-Sagittaire.* 1960. Tapestry, 7'1⅞" × 9'11" (2.2 × 3.05 m). Courtesy Madame Lurçat, Paris.

b Helga and Bent Exner. Brooch in white gold and tugtupite, created for H.R.H. Queen Ingrid of Denmark, c. 1972.

c Maurice Utrillo. *Church of Le Sacré Coeur, Montmartre et Rue Saint-Rustique* N.d. Oil on canvas, 19½ × 24" (49 × 61 cm). Museum of Fine Arts, Boston (bequest of John T. Spaulding).

d Dirk Bouts. *Last Supper Altarpiece,* detail. 1464–67. Panel, 6' × 5'⅛" (1.83 × 1.53 m). Church of St.-Pierre, Louvain.

a

b

c

d

Balance

Crystallographic Balance

Allover Pattern

One more specific type of visual effect is often designated as a fourth variety of balance. The examples here illustrate the idea. These works all exhibit an equal emphasis over the whole format—the same weight or eye attraction literally everywhere. This is officially called *crystallographic balance.* Since few people can remember this term, and even fewer can spell it, the more common name is *allover pattern.* This is, of course, a rather special refinement of symmetrical balance. But the constant repetition of the same quality everywhere on the surface *is* truly a different impression from our usual concept of symmetrical balance.

Lee Krasner's nonobjective expressionist painting *Polar Stampede* **(a)** has a dynamic pattern that extends without real change over the whole painting. There is no beginning, no end, and no focal point—unless, indeed, the whole picture is the focal point.

In Jasper Johns' painting **(b)** there is again uniform emphasis throughout. The many numbers appear in the same size with each defined in the same loose, fluid brushstroke and paint texture. Value changes are interesting, but are also quite evenly distributed.

Fabric patterns, with their purposeful lack of any focal point, are usually distinguished by a constant repetition of the same motif **(c).**

Sculpture may also, at times, employ crystallographic balance. Ibram Lassaw's linear pattern **(d)** in bronze and steel is not a repetition of identical elements. But the rather free rectangular forms repeat everywhere, and the areas of emphasis (where the forms become smaller and more complicated) are distributed evenly throughout the design. Again, with every area equally stressed, no focal point occurs.

---

a Lee Krasner. *Polar Stampede.* 1960. Oil on canvas, 7′9⅝″ × 13′3¾″ (2.37 × 4.06 m). Collection Lee Krasner.

b Jasper Johns. *Numbers in Color.* 1959. Encaustic and newspaper on canvas, 5′6½″ × 4′1⅛″ (1.69 × 1.26 m). Albright-Knox Art Gallery, Buffalo, NY (gift of Seymour H. Knox, 1959).

c In some instances, as in fabric patterns, a focal point is deliberately excluded.

d Ibram Lassaw. *Clouds of Magellan.* 1953. Welded bronze and steel. 4′4″ × 5′10″ × 1′6″ (1.32 × 1.78 × 0.46 m). Collection Philip Johnson, New York.

a

b

c

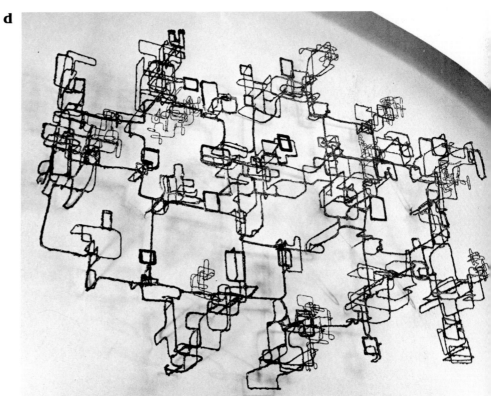

d

4

Scale/ Proportion

Scale and *proportion* are similar terms with a slightly different emphasis. *Scale* refers essentially to size; "large scale" is a way of saying big, and "small scale" means small. "Big" and "small," however, are relative. What is big? Big is meaningless unless we have some standard of reference. A *big* dog means nothing if we do not know the size of most dogs. This is what separates the two terms. *Proportion* refers to *relative* size, size measured against other elements or against some mental norm or standard. Look at the design in **a**. Here the large black circle would

certainly be called large scale. It is a large element and occupies much space, given the overall dimensions of the design. It could also be described as out of *proportion*. Compared to the other, tiny elements, it is *too* large and overwhelms the rest of the pattern, demanding all our visual attention. The phrase *out of scale* could also be applied to the big circle, implying the same fault. An out-of-scale element in a work is not always a fault. Depending on the purpose of the artist, such an element could communicate a theme, however visually disturbing.

Scale and proportion are closely tied to emphasis and focal point. Large scale and especially large size in proportion to other elements make for an obvious visual emphasis. In **b** the eye goes naturally first to the large-scale figure in the center. The artist, Honoré Sharrer, has created a focal point that dominates the other small figures in the windows of the building in the background.

In past centuries, visual scale was often related to thematic importance. The size of figures was based on their symbolic importance in the subject being presented. In the 11th-century illumination (**c**), the angel appearing to the shepherds is drawn unnaturally large. The artist thus immediately established not only an obvious visual focal point but also indicated the angel's religious conceptual importance. This use of size is called *hieratic scaling.*

---

a The large circle, out of proportion to the other elements, overwhelms them.

b Honoré Sharrer. *The Industrial Scene,* center panel of *Tribute to the American Working People.* 1945–50. Oil on canvas, 25 × 31" (63 × 79 cm). Whereabouts unknown.

c *Annunciation to the Shepherds,* from the Gospel lectionary of Henry II. c. 1002–24. Manuscript illumination, 13 × 9⅜" (33 × 24 cm). Bayerische Staatsbibliothek, Munich.

a

Scale of Art

Scale/Proportion

There are two ways to think of artistic scale. One is to consider the scale of the work itself—its size in relation to other art, in relation to its surroundings, or in relation to human size. Unhappily, the one thing book illustrations cannot do is show art in its original size or scale. Unusual or unexpected scale is arresting and attention getting. Sheer size *does* impress us.

When we are confronted by frescoes such as the Sistine Chapel ceiling, our first reaction is simply awe at the enormous scope of the work. Later, we study and admire details, but first we are overwhelmed by the sheer magnitude. The reverse effect is illustrated in **a**. It comes as a shock to stand before this actual painting, for it is tiny, 5 by 5¾ inches—barely larger than its reproduction here. The exquisite detail, the delicate pre-

cision of the drawing, and the color subtleties all impress us. Our first thought has to be of the fantastic difficulty of achieving such effects in so tiny a format.

If large or small size springs naturally from the function, theme, or purpose of a work, an unusual scale is justified. We are acquainted with many such cases. The gigantic pyramids made a political statement of the Pharaoh's eternal power. The ele-

gant miniatures of the religious book of hours (**b**) served as book illustrations for the private devotionals of medieval nobility. The small, detailed golden saltcellar (**c**) graced a regal dining table. The scale of Kent Twitchell's enormous (40 feet high) wall painting (**d**) dwarfs even today's large billboards. The naturalistic images blown up to such monumental scale cannot be ignored, and they alter the urban environment.

a Follower of Jan van Eyck. *St. Francis Receiving the Stigmata.* Early 15th century. Oil on panel, 5 × 5¾" (13 × 15 cm). Galleria Sabauda, Turin.
b Limbourg Brothers. *Multiplication of the Loaves and Fishes,* from the Book of Hours (*Les Très Riches Heures*) of the Duke of Berry. 1416. Manuscript illumination, 6¼ × 4⅜" (16 × 11 cm). Musée Condé, Chantilly.
c Benvenuto Cellini. The saltcellar of Francis I. 1539–43. Gold, 10¼ × 13" (26 × 33 cm). Kunsthistorisches Museum, Vienna.
d Kent Twitchell. *The Holy Trinity with the Virgin.* 1977–78. Acrylic wall painting, 40 × 56' (12.2 × 17.1 m). Otis/Parsons Art Institute, Los Angeles.

d

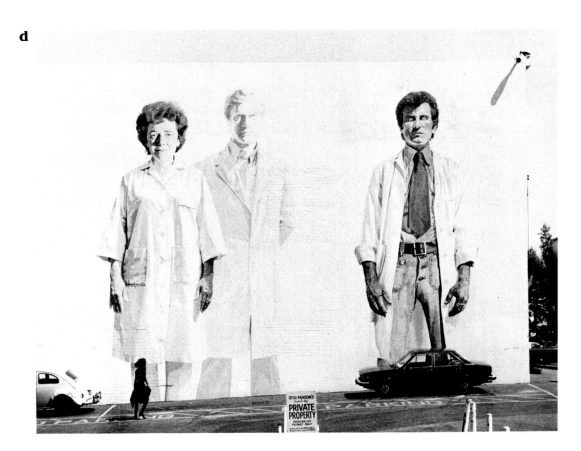

Scale/Proportion

Scale of Art

The Bulgarian-born artist Christo has conceived and constructed unique landscape projects that are truly gigantic in scale. His *Valley Curtain* hung an orange curtain between two mountains in Colorado. A fence was built that ran over 24 miles of rolling hills in suburban California. The sheer scale of such works was impressive. A recent project has involved islands in a bay in Florida **(a)**. Eleven islands were surrounded by wide pink fabric bands (or "skirts" as some observers dubbed them). Again, the scope of the project was tremendous, involving 6½ million square feet of floating fabric. Whether viewed from a boat or from the air, observers saw a familiar landscape environment in a suddenly new and altered context. Public controversy often accompanies these projects, although one could argue a traditional link to the past in the huge earthworks constructed in many countries by ancient peoples.

Probably no motif from contemporary art has been reproduced so many times for so many different purposes as Robert Indiana's *Love* **(b)**. It has been the decorative theme of T-shirts, coffee mugs, matchbook covers, wall posters, bracelet charms, postage stamps, cocktail napkins, and myriad other things. In each medium, it has changed scale; but each time it remained graphically appealing to a large audience. That it can be effective in so many different sizes and contexts would seem to be proof of the image's absolute brilliance or utter fatuousness.

Unusual scale in a work of art should have a thematic or functional justification. Bigness for the sake of bigness, simply to gain attention, is usually a mistake. French salon artists of the 19th century often painted their illustrative anecdotes in enormous scale in order to stand out among the hundreds of works shown in the yearly exhibits. This is understandable, but when viewed individually, the huge scale makes the emptiness and pretentiousness of the work all the more painfully obvious. Example **c** is a sentimental, trivial scene. Did it truly *need* to be almost 5 feet by 4 feet in size? Be sure you know in your mind *why* your design should be overlarge or very tiny.

a Christo, *Surrounded Islands*. 1980–83. Biscayne Bay, Greater Miami, FLA.
© 1980–83 Christo/C.V.J. Corporation.
b Robert Indiana. *Love*. 1968. Aluminum. 12 × 12 × 6″ (30 × 30 × 15 cm). Whitney Museum of American Art, New York (gift of the Howard and Jean Lipman Foundation, Inc.).
c Adolphe Bouguereau. *The Thank Offering*. 1867. Oil on canvas, 4′10″ × 3′6¼″ (1.47 × 1.07 m). Philadelphia Museum of Art (Wilstach Collection, given by John G. Johnson).

a

b

c

Scale/Proportion

Scale within Art

The second way to discuss artistic scale is to consider the size and scale of elements *within* the design or pattern. The scale here, of course, is relative to the overall area of the format; a big element in one painting might be small in a larger work.

The three examples in **a** show how variations in scale can yield very different design effects. Having elements of differing sizes brings visual interest and, as you can see, affects the emphasis. Which design is "best"

or which we prefer can be argued. The answer would depend upon what effect we wish to create.

Look at the difference scale can make in a painting. Examples **b** and **c** both have themes dealing with the sufferings of Christ. In Tintoretto's painting **(b)** of the Crucifixion, tiny figures crowd the scene, and Christ is small scale, barely identifiable. Tintoretto gives us a vast panorama of events. We see the thieves being crucified with Christ, the soldiers

gambling for His robe, the mob—all the various facets of the story. Painting **c**, by the 20th-century artist Rouault, is in a very different style. But probably the main difference in the two images is the use of scale within the picture. In contrast to the Tintoretto **(b)**, Rouault's figure of Christ being mocked by the soldiers is large scale. The two background figures of Roman soldiers give a suggestion of the larger story, but we concentrate on the personal agony of Christ. Because of the large scale of Christ, we forget all the other elements and focus on His sorrowful attitude. Both paintings are emotional images, but the scale of the elements results in contrasting impressions.

a Changes in scale within a design also change the total effect.
b Jacopo Tintoretto. *The Crucifixion.* 1565. Oil on canvas, 17'7" × 40'2" (5.36 × 12.24 m). Sala dell'Albergo, Scuola di San Rocco, Venice.
c Georges Rouault. *Christ Mocked by Soldiers.* 1932. Oil on canvas, 36¼ × 28½" (92 × 72 cm). Museum of Modern Art, New York (anonymous gift).

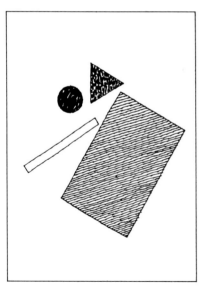 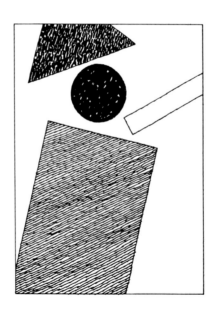 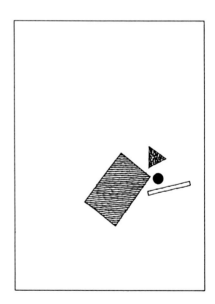

a

Scale Within Art

Scale/Proportion

Scale can attract our attention in different ways, depending on the artist's purpose. Scale can also be used to draw our notice to the unexpected or exaggerated, as when small objects are magnified or large ones reduced. The American artist Georgia O'Keefe took the blossoms of roses and a calla lily and enlarged them to a canvas-filling scale **(a)**. The delicate small flowers become a monumental image 4 feet wide.

Photographers often exploit the use of an extreme close-up view to produce an unusual, dramatic image out of perhaps prosaic subject matter. The Paul Strand photograph of a car **(b)**, dating from 1917, is an example. The shadows and reflections on the large forms contrasted with the linear spokes of the wheel create an almost abstract design.

Painter Jim Dine took the opposite approach to scale **(c)**. In a large pencil-and-watercolor drawing, six toothbrushes are isolated in a vast empty area. Now the deliberate small scale provides the interest.

Both techniques of unexpectedly large or unusually small images are often used by designers of advertising. The change from the usual, or expected, scale can attract the casual reader's attention.

a Georgia O'Keeffe. *Calla Lily with Red Roses.* 1927. Oil on canvas, 2'6" × 4' (0.76 × 1.22 m). Private collection.
b Paul Strand. *Wheel 2 Mudguard.* 1917. Platinum print, 12⅝ × 10" (32 × 25 cm). Metropolitan Museum of Art, New York (Alfred Stieglitz Collection, 1944, Naef 523).
c Jim Dine. *Six Toothbrushes, Number 1.* 1962. Pencil and watercolor on paper, 29 × 23" (74 × 58 cm). Whitney Museum of American Art, New York (purchase).

c

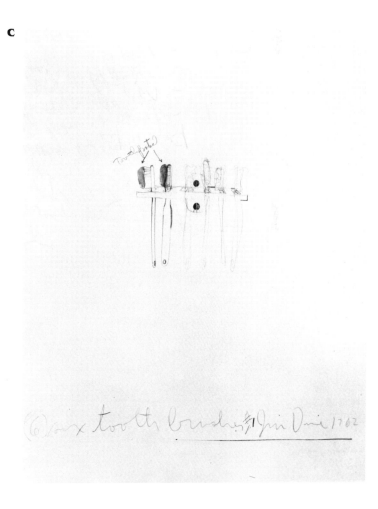

Scale/Proportion

Scale Confusion

The deliberate changing of natural scale is not unusual in painting. In religious paintings many artists have arbitrarily increased the size of the Christ or Virgin figure to emphasize philosophic and religious importance.

Some artists, however, use scale changes intentionally to intrigue or mystify us, rather than to clarify the focal point. Figure **a** is an unusual painting by the American artist Erastus Field. In viewing it, we are struck immediately by the image of this impossibly enormous building. The many tall towers, the almost countless colonnades, the statuary—all in a veritable maze of architectural details—combine to create a truly incredible building. Some tiny figures and some trees in the foreground set the gigantic scale. The artist has painted a vision, an image totally outside our experience.

Surrealism is an art form based on paradox, on images that cannot be explained in rational terms. Artists who work in this manner present the irrational world of the dream or nightmare—recognizable elements in impossible situations. The painting by Magritte (**b**) shows one such enigma, with much of the mystery stemming from a confusion of scale. We identify the various elements easily enough, but they are all the "wrong" size and strange in proportion to each other. Does the painting show an impossibly large comb, shaving brush, bar of soap, and other items, or are these items normal sized but placed in a doll's house room? Neither explanation makes rational sense.

The Dada artists also used irrational imagery. The photomontage in **c**, by Hannah Höch, again employs scale differences to produce a totally incongruous design. The extreme shifts in size on various parts of the two dancers startle and intrigue the viewer.

a Erastus Salisbury Field. *Historical Monument of the American Republic.* c. 1876. Oil on canvas, 9'3" × 13'1" (2.82 × 3.99 m). Museum of Fine Arts, Springfield, MA (Morgan Wesson Memorial Collection).

b René Magritte. *Personal Values.* 1952. Oil on canvas, 31⅝ × 39½" (80 × 100 cm). Collection Harry Torczyner, New York.

c Hannah Höch. *Dada Dance.* 1919–21. Photomontage, 12⅝ × 9" (32 × 23 cm). Berlinische Galerie, West Berlin.

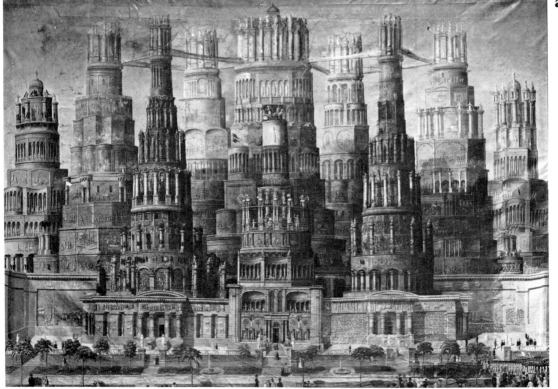
a

b

c

Der Höllenüberschuß fällt in die Kaffe des Pfarrers Klatt

für unschuldige Verbrecherkinder

DADA-TANZ   H. Höch 19

5

Illusion
of Space

Illusion of Space

Several art forms are three-dimensional and therefore occupy space: ceramics, jewelry and metalwork, weaving, and sculpture, to name a few. In traditional sculpture or in a purely abstract pattern of forms such as Louise Bourgeois' work **(a)**, it is important for us to move about and enjoy the changing spatial patterns from various angles. Architecture, of course, is an art form mainly preoccupied with the enclosure of three-dimensional space.

In two-dimensional art forms such as drawing, painting, and prints, the artist often desires to convey a feeling of space or depth. Here space is merely an illusion, for the images rendered on paper, canvas, or board are essentially flat.

This illusion of space is an option for the artist. Painting **b**, by Jean Dewasne, is a dynamic pattern of shapes that remain flat on the *picture plane*, the frontal plane of the painting. Nothing encourages us to see

"back" into the composition. On the other hand, the Victorian artist Edith Hayller's painting **(c)** pierces the picture plane. We are encouraged to forget that a painting is merely a flat piece of canvas. Instead, we are almost standing in the very room, looking into another farther room, and seeing the garden through a distant window. Hayller's images suggest three-dimensional forms in a area full of air and "real" space. The picture plane no longer exists as a plane, but becomes a "window" into a simulated three-dimensional world created by the artist. A very convincing illusion is created. Many artists, through the centuries, have studied this problem of presenting a visual illusion of space and depth. Several devices have been used.

a Louise Bourgeois. *Femme Maison '81.* 1981. Marble, 4'⅛" × 3'11" × 4'1⅞" (1.22 × 1.19 × 1.27 m). Robert Miller Gallery, New York.

b Jean Dewasne. *La Demeure Antipode.* 1965. Enamel on masonite, 3'1⅞" × 4'2⅞" (0.96 × 1.29 m). Solomon R. Guggenheim Museum, New York (gift of Herbert C. Bernard).

c Edith Hayller. *A Summer Shower.* 1883. Oil on board, 20 × 16¾" (51 × 43 cm). Forbes Magazine Collection, New York.

a

b

c

Illusion of Space

Devices to Show Depth

Size

The easiest way to create an illusion of space or distance is through *size*. Very early in life, we observe the visual phenomenon that as objects get farther away, they appear to become smaller. Thus, when we look at the subway scene by George Tooker (**a**), we see the differences in size of the various figures. This immediately establishes a sense of pictorial space. We know the smaller figures are not tiny midgets, but are simply farther away from us down the various corridors.

In Hobbema's landscape painting (**b**), the repeating forms of the trees gradually diminish in size and effectively lead us back into space, creating a very deep painting with the small-scale town far in the distance.

Notice that the size factor can be effective even with abstract shapes, where the forms have no literal meaning or representational quality (**c**). The smaller squares automatically begin to recede, and we see a spatial pattern. With abstract figures, the spatial effect is more pronounced if (as in **c**) the same shape is repeated in various sizes. The device works less well with different shapes.

Artists in the past sometimes ignored size as a way to show spatial location. Size was often used to denote some conceptual importance and not to indicate how close or far away the figure was spatially. This is called *hieratic scaling.* Thus, deities, angels, and rulers might be shown in an arbitrarily large size to indicate their thematic importance.

a George Tooker. *The Subway.* 1950. Egg tempera on composition board, 18 × 36″ (46 × 92 cm). Whitney Museum of Art, New York (Juliana Force purchase).
b Meindert Hobbema. *Avenue at Middelharnis.* 1689. Oil on canvas, 3′4¾″ × 4′7½″ (1.04 × 1.41 m). National Gallery, London (reproduced by courtesy of the Trustees).
c If the same shape is repeated in different sizes, a spatial effect can be achieved.

a

b

c

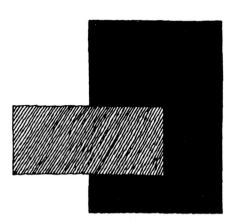

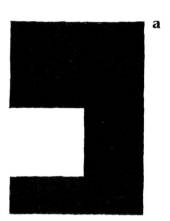

a

b

c

Devices to Show Depth

Illusion of Space

Overlapping

Overlapping is a simple device for creating an illusion of depth. When you look at the two rectangles in **a** you do not assume that the black shape is missing a piece, as shown at the right. Instead, you realize that the gray shape is hiding part of the black rectangle because it is on top of or in front of it, thereby automatically creating a sense of depth.

In the detail of Fra Angelico's painting **(b)**, the rows of saints are shown with no size difference between the figures in the front row and those in back. But we do understand their respective positions because of the overlapping that hides portions of the figures in the second and third rows. Since overlapping is the only spatial device used, the space created is admittedly very shallow, and we get a "stacked-up" feeling. Notice that when overlapping is combined with size differences, as in Perugino's painting **(c)**, the spatial sensation is greatly increased.

The same principle can be illustrated with abstract shapes, as the designs in **d** show. The design at the right, which combines overlapping and size differences, gives a much more effective feeling of spatial recession.

---

a Overlapping establishes a feeling of depth in a design.
b Fra Angelico. *Christ Glorified in the Court of Heaven*, detail. 1435. Panel, detail 12½ × 25″ (32 × 64 cm). National Gallery, London (reproduced by courtesy of the Trustees).
c Pietro Perugino. *The Delivery of the Keys to St. Peter.* 1482. Fresco. Sistine Chapel, The Vatican, Rome.
d The design at the left does not give as much feeling of spatial depth as the one on the right.

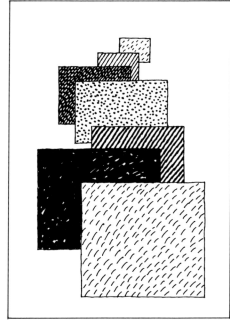

Illusion of Space

Devices to Show Depth

Transparency

Many artists in the 20th century have chosen to ignore the device of overlapping. Instead, they have used what is called *transparency*. When two forms overlap and both are seen completely, the figures are assumed to be transparent (**a**).

Transparency does *not* give us a clear spatial pattern. In **a** we are not sure which form is on top and which behind. The spatial pattern can change as we look at it. This pur-poseful ambiguity is called *equivocal space*, and many artists find it a more interesting visual pattern than the immediately clear spatial organization provided by overlapping in a design.

There is another rationale for the use of transparency. Just because one item is in front and hides another object does not mean the item in back has ceased to exist. In **b** a bowl of fruit is depicted with the customary visual device of overlapping. In **c** the same bowl of fruit is shown with transparency, and we discover that other pieces of fruit are in the bottom of the bowl. They were always there, but hidden from our view. Which design is more "realistic"? By what standard do you decide?

Cubism was an art style primarily interested in studying form. Cubist artists often used transparency (**d**) because they felt the contrast and relationship of various shapes was more effective when each was seen entirely, instead of being partially hidden by the momentary accident of overlapping.

The print by Norman Ives (**e**) is an arrangement of the block shapes of sans-serif letters (letters without decorative "tails"). However, the use of transparency on all the overlapping letters creates many *new* shapes, and their light and dark changes create an interesting pattern.

a The use of overlapping with transparency confuses our perception of depth.
b Overlapping sometimes can be deceptive.
c The use of transparency reveals what is hidden by overlapping.
d Juan Gris. *Still Life Before an Open Window: Place Ravignan.* 1915. Oil on canvas, 44¾ × 35" (114 × 89 cm). Philadelphia Museum of Art (Louise and Walter Arensberg Collection).
e Norman Ives. *I: Centaur.* 1973. Serigraph, 22" (56 cm) square. Estate of Norman Ives.

a

b

c

d

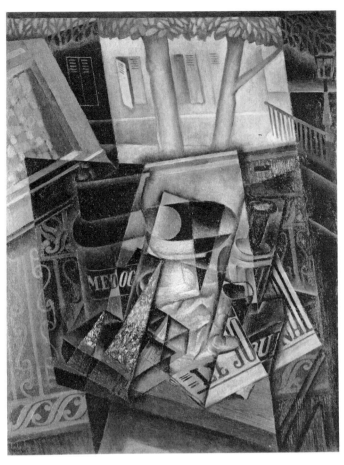

e

Devices to Show Depth

Illusion of Space

Vertical Location

Vertical location is a spatial device in which elevation on the page or format indicates a recession into depth. The *higher* an object, the farther back it is assumed to be. In the Persian miniature **(a)**, the various figures and objects are depicted with no differences in size, but with some overlapping. The artist is relying mainly on vertical location to give us a sense of recession into depth. This spatial device was used widely in Near Eastern art and often in Oriental art and was immediately understandable in those cultures.

These examples are charming and decorative, but to Western eyes they have little spatial depth. To us, the figures appear almost to sit on top of each other all in one plane. However, if vertical location is combined with a size difference, it provides a very effective feeling of space. In Andrew Wyeth's painting **(b)** the distance between the figure and the smaller house is emphatically heightened by the placement of the house at the top of the picture. The isolation of the figure is strongly dramatized by the distance created.

Vertical location is based on a visual fact. As we stand and look at the scene before us, the closest place to us is the ground down at our feet. As we gradually raise our eyes upward, objects move farther away until we reach what is called the *horizon,* or eye level. Thus, a horizon reference is an integral part of vertical location. In the 20th century, we have gained the ability to fly, and the traditional ground-horizon-sky visual reference has been considerably altered. We are increasingly accustomed to images such as **c**, where the traditional "horizon" has disappeared and the point farthest from us is now toward the bottom of the picture. Vertical location is still an effective spatial device but not as automatically effective as in the past.

---

a *Bahram Gur in the Turquoise Palace on Wednesday.* 16th century. Persian miniature. Metropolitan Museum of Art, New York (gift of Alexander Smith Cochran, 1913).
b Andrew Wyeth. *Christina's World.* 1948. Tempera on gesso panel, 32¼ × 47¾" (82 × 121 cm). Museum of Modern Art, New York (purchase).
c Berenice Abbott. *Wall Street, Showing East River, from Roof of Irving Trust Company.* 1938. Photograph. Museum of the City of New York.

c

a

b

c

Devices to Show Depth

Illusion of Space

Aerial Perspective

Aerial, or *atmospheric, perspective* means the use of color and/or value (dark and light) to show depth. Example **a** illustrates the idea: the value contrast between distant objects gradually lessens, and contours become less distinct. The color would change also, with objects that are far away appearing more neutral in color and taking on a bluish character.

In **b** the feeling of spatial recession is based entirely on differences in size. Example **c** shows the same design, but the spatial feeling is greatly increased, since the smaller shapes become progressively darker and show less value contrast with the background.

In George Robson's 19th-century watercolor (**d**), the artist uses gradually lessening value contrasts to establish the sense of the buildings receding farther and farther away. The sharper value contrasts in the foreground figures (boats, stones, etc.) pull these items visually forward. The wall at the bottom left is sharply delineated in detail and value.

a Ansel Adams. *Yosemite Valley from Inspiration Point.* c. 1936. Photograph.
b A feeling of spatial recession can be achieved simply by reducing the size of objects as they apparently fade into the distance.
c Spatial recession can be made even more effective if the receding objects blend more and more with the background.
d George Fennel Robson. *St. Paul's from Southwark by Sunset.* 1833. Watercolor and body color over pencil, 24 × 36″ (68 × 92 cm). Yale Center for British Art, New Haven, CT (Paul Mellon Fund).

d

a

b

c

Devices to Show Depth

Illusion of Space

Linear Perspective

Linear perspective is a complex spatial system based on a relatively simple visual phenomenon: as parallel lines recede, they appear to converge and to meet on an imaginary line called the *horizon,* or *eye level.* We have all noticed this effect with railroad tracks or a highway stretching away into the distance, as painting **a** illustrates. From this obvious visual effect, the whole "science" of linear perspective has developed. Artists had long noted this convergence of receding parallel lines, but not until the Renaissance was the idea introduced that parallel lines on parallel planes all converge at the same place (a *vanishing point*) on the horizon. Thus, in de Hooch's painting **(b)** all the lines of windows, walls, floor tiles, and ceiling beams, if ex-

tended, would meet at a common point **(c)**.

Linear perspective was a dominant device for spatial representation in Western art for several hundred years. It is easy to see why. First, linear perspective does approximate the visual image; it does appear "realistic" for artists striving to reproduce what the eye sees. Second, by its very nature, perspective acts as a unifying factor. With all the lines receding to a common point, it auto-

matically organizes these many trapezoidal shapes into a coherent pattern. Look at Leonardo da Vinci's *The Last Supper* **(d)**. The one-point perspective not only visually unites the two walls, their dark panels, the lines of the coffered ceiling, and so forth, but the vanishing point placed at Christ's head draws our eyes to this focal point. So perfect are the compositional clarity and unified spatial organization that the painting has become almost a cliché.

d

Illusion of Space

Devices to Show Depth

Linear Perspective

The complete study of linear perspective is a complicated task. Whole books are devoted to it alone, and it cannot be fully described here. However, a quick glance at the illustrations will enable you to recognize some different perspective systems.

In the drawing *Urban Blast* (**a**), the tiny figure is about to blow up a vast array of buildings shown in what is referred to as *one-point perspective*.

On each of the buildings we can see one side that is parallel to the picture plane, and then the other side diminishes in size as it recedes. All the lines on the different buildings recede to one common vanishing point.

When we look at the corner of a room or building, so that no planes are parallel to the picture plane, *two-point perspective* results. You can see in Edward Ruscha's painting (**b**) that the lines of the gas station, if

extended, would meet at two different, widely spaced vanishing points, the left one outside the picture. Since two-point perspective approximates people's usual visual experience, it is used a great deal in interior and architectural renderings of design proposals.

Artists often use what is called *multipoint perspective,* in which several different vanishing points on the horizon are employed. The painting by Ronald Davis (**c**) shows multipoint perspective used in an abstract manner.

The rules and "engineering" aspects of linear perspective have led many 20th-century artists away from its use, to reliance on other forms of spatial definition. Linear perspective is merely a tool for artists to employ when appropriate or to ignore when they wish.

a Hans-Georg Rauch. *Urban Blast.* 1966. Pen and ink, 17½ × 12½" (45 × 32 cm). Courtesy the artist.

b Edward Ruscha. *Standard Station, Amarillo, Texas.* 1963. Oil on canvas, 5'5" × 10'4" (1.65 × 3.15 m). Hood Museum of Art, Dartmouth College, Hanover, NH.

c Ronald Davis. *Frame and Beam.* 1975. Acrylic and dry pigment, 9'4" × 15'4½" (2.9 × 4.73 m). Seattle Art Museum (purchased with funds from National Endowment for the Arts, Poncho, and Merrill Foundation).

a

b

c

a

b

Devices to Show Depth

Illusion of Space

Limitations of Linear Perspective

Linear perspective approximates what our eyes see, but its limitations have made it less popular in the 20th century than in preceding periods.

Many artists object to the restraints that perspective implies. The artist's compositional freedom consists of the placement of the horizon, vanishing points, and the first line. Then the composition becomes a mechanical drawing exercise in following rules.

The main objection is the "frozen" quality that linear perspective imparts. With required unchanging horizon line and vanishing points, a perspective drawing suggests a stoppage of time; we are staring at a scene without movement. This is not what we experience in life, for our visual knowledge is gained by looking at objects or scenes from many changing viewpoints. Example **a** is a photo of a room from a fixed viewpoint—a "true" view if we came in, stopped completely, and stared at the room without moving our eyes. This, however, is a limited perspective and not true to life. In **b**, a composite photo, the camera was focused on several parts of the room individually, and the results combined into one composition. This image more closely approximates our visual experience as our eyes move from one item to another, looking at each in turn.

This changing aspect of perception is obviously what Renato Guttuso was attempting in **c**. Rather than taking one fixed view, the artist shows different figures from different angles to suggest the effect of moving along a beach.

a Linear perspective can show only one viewpoint at one moment.
b In reality, our eyes move from one object to another, combining many images to make a composite whole.
c Renato Guttuso. *The Beach.* 1955. Oil on canvas, 9'9⅜" × 14'8¼" (3.01 × 4.52 m). Galleria Nazionale, Parma.

c

Illusion of Space

Amplified Perspective

To introduce a dramatic, dynamic quality into their pictures, many artists have used what is called *amplified perspective.* This device reproduces the visual image, but in the very special view that occurs when an item is pointed directly at the viewer.

A familiar example is James Montgomery Flagg's recruiting poster of Uncle Sam **(a)**, in which the pointing finger is thrust right at the viewer and the arm recedes sharply. This effect is called *foreshortening.* Because the arm points right at us, it looks "shorter" than we know it to be. In profile, of course, the arm would look much longer.

In Dali's painting of the Crucifixion **(b)**, the body of Christ is also foreshortened. We look from above the cross so that the body very quickly recedes down and away from us, rapidly getting smaller. It is an unusual view, and the size contrast of large to small is pictorially exciting.

Another advantage of amplified perspective is that the viewer's eye is pulled quickly into the picture. In Rubens' painting **(c)**, the figure of Prometheus thrust diagonally at us exerts a dynamic pull inward, avoiding the static, frozen quality of so many works. With amplified perspective, the spatial quality becomes the image's most eye-catching element. It is an effective tool in making the viewer forget that the picture is a flat, two-dimensional plane.

a James Montgomery Flagg. *I Want YOU.* World War I recruiting poster. Library of Congress, Washington, DC.
b Salvador Dali. *Christ of St. John of the Cross.* 1951. Oil on canvas, 6'8⅝" × 3'9⅝" (2.05 × 1.16 m). Glasgow Art Gallery (purchased 1952).
c Peter Paul Rubens. *Prometheus Bound.* 1611–12. Oil on canvas, 7'11⅞" × 6'10½" (2.44 × 2.1 m). Philadelphia Museum of Art (purchase, W. P. Wilstach Collection).

a

b

c

a

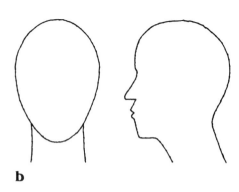

b

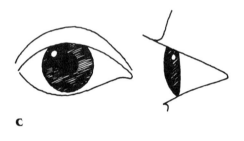

c

d

Multiple Perspective

Illusion of Space

Looking at a figure or object from more than one vantage point simultaneously is called *multiple perspective*. Several different views are combined in one image. This device has been used widely in 20th-century art, although the idea is centuries old.

Multiple perspective was a basic pictorial device in Egyptian art, as illustrated in a typical Egyptian painted figure (**a**). The artist's aim was not necessarily to reproduce the visual image, but to give a composite image combining the most descriptive or characteristic view of each part of the body. In **b**, which view of the head is most descriptive, which most certainly a head? The profile obviously says "head" more clearly. But what about the eye (**c**)? The eye in profile is a confusing shape, but the front view is what we know as an eye. The Egyptians solved this problem by combining a side view of the head with a front view of the eye. Each body part is thus presented in

its most characteristic aspect: a front view of the torso, a side view of the legs, and so forth.

Multiple perspective was widely used also in Near Eastern and Indian art. Notice the pool and fountain in the Indian picture (**d**).

In the 20th century, with the camera able to give us effortlessly the fixed visual ("realistic") view, artists have been freed to explore other avenues of perception including multiple perspective. The Cubist artist Braque clearly employed multiple perspective in his still life (**e**). We look down on the top of the table to see more clearly the items collected

there. But the table is as important as the objects (the picture is entitled *The Round Table*), and it would be a pity not to see the delightful old-fashioned base and curved legs. So we see them from the side. The items themselves, while *abstracted* or simplified into basic shapes, are shown from differing angles to give us the most descriptive view, or views, of each individual item.

As you have noticed, multiple perspective does not give a clear spatial pattern of the position occupied by each element. This aspect has been sacrificed to give a more subjective, conceptual view of forms.

---

a *The Sculptor Apuy and His Wife*, detail of Egyptian wall painting (restored). c. 1275 B.C. Tomb of Apuy, Deir el Medina. Metropolitan Museum of Art, New York.

b To the Egyptians, the head shown in profile seemed to be the most characteristic view.

c The *front* view of the eye gives the clearest, most descriptive view.

d *Ladies in a Pleasure Garden*, detail. c. 1675–1700. Manuscript illumination from Bundi, India, 12 × 8¾" (30 × 22 cm). Courtesy of the Trustees of the Prince of Wales Museum of Western India, Bombay.

e Georges Braque. *The Round Table (Le Grand Gueridon)*. 1929. Oil on canvas, 4'10" × 3'9" (1.47 × 1.14 m). Phillips Collection, Washington, DC.

e

a

b

c

d

Oriental Space

Isometric Projection

For centuries, Oriental artists did not make wide use of linear perspective. Another spatial convention was satisfactory for their pictorial purposes. In Oriental art, planes recede on the diagonal, but the lines, instead of drawing closer together, remain parallel. Example **a** shows a box drawn in linear perspective, **b** the box drawn in the Oriental method. In the West, we refer to image **b** as an isometric projection.

A typical Japanese print (**c**) illustrates this device. The effect is different, but certainly not disturbing. For one thing, the space is already very shallow; the corner of the room is not far from the picture plane. The rather flat decorative effect seems perfectly in keeping with the treatment of the figures, with their strong linear pattern and flat color areas. The artist does not stress three-dimensional solidity or roundness in the figures, so we do not miss this quality in the background.

In fact, when linear perspective *is* used by an Oriental artist, as in **d**, the effect can be quite unsatisfactory. The same flat figures now look strange in a deep space—like the pop-up figures in children's books.

Oriental art rarely stressed the strictly visual impression of the world. The art was more subjective, more evocative than descriptive of the natural world. Linear perspective was undoubtedly not needed for the expressive aims of these artists.

Isometric projection, while used extensively in engineering and mechanical drawings, is rarely seen in Western painting. But a visual change from the more common linear perspective can be fresh and intriguing, as the 19th-century American folk-art painting in **e** illustrates.

a In linear perspective, parallel lines gradually draw closer together as they recede in the distance.

b In isometric projection, parallel lines remain parallel.

c Torii Kiyomasu I. *An Oiran with Two Kamuro Stopping in the Street.* c. 1715. Japanese print, 11 × 16″ (28 × 41 cm). Metropolitan Museum of Art, New York (Harris Brisbane Dick Fund, 1949).

d Furuyama Moromasa. *Game of Hand Sumō.* c. 1740. Woodcut, 13 × 18½″ (33 × 47 cm). Metropolitan Museum of Art, New York (Frederick C. Hewitt Fund, 1912).

e American School. *Mahantango Valley Farm.* Late 19th century. Window shade, 28 × 35⅜″ (71 × 90 cm). National Gallery of Art, Washington, DC (gift of Edgar William and Bernice Chrysler Garbisch, 1953).

Illusion of Space

Open Form/Closed Form

One other aspect of pictorial space is of concern to the artist or designer. This is the concept of *enclosure*, the use of what is referred to as *open form* or *closed form*. The artist has the choice of giving us a complete scene or merely a partial glimpse of a portion of a scene that continues beyond the format. In **a** Fragonard has enclosed the focal point, and our eyes are not led out of the painting. The inward-facing statue and the mass of trees at left frame the lovers in the center and effectively keep our attention focused on them. This is called *closed form*.

By contrast, example **b** is clearly *open form*. In Clayton Pond's humorous serigraph, only partial glimpses of the figure are seen, and all these lead the eye *off* the format. In fact, this design almost forces us to think more of the parts we *cannot* see than of those shown in the picture.

The ultimate extension of the open form concept is illustrated in **c**. This large nonobjective painting by Jasper Johns has a shape that really does protrude outside the rectangle of the painting. The shape both surprises us and effectively destroys any "framed," or contained, feeling in the format.

We do generally frame paintings; a frame is a border around the perimeter that visually turns the eye inward. Thus, frames create the effect of closed form, no matter what the original design of the artwork. Some artists have gone even further and included painted "frames" (and even lettered titles) as elements within the composition (**d**).

As you can see, closed form generally gives a rather formal, structured appearance, while open form creates a casual, momentary feeling with elements moving on and off the format in an informal manner.

a Jean-Honoré Fragonard. *The Love Letters*. 1771–73. Oil on canvas, 10'4⅞" × 7'1⅜" (3.17 × 2.17 m). Frick Collection, New York (copyright).

b Clayton Pond. *Self-Portrait in the Bathtub*, from the series *Things in My Studio*. 1973. Screenprint, 23 × 29" (58 × 74 cm). Courtesy Associated American Artists, New York.

c Jasper Johns. *Studio*. 1964. Oil on canvas, 6'1½" × 12'1½" (1.87 × 3.7 m). Whitney Museum of American Art, New York (gift of the Friends of the Whitney Museum of American Art and purchase).

d Neil Jenny. *North America Abstracted*. 1980. Oil on wood, 3'¼" × 7'1¼" (0.92 × 2.17 m). Whitney Museum of American Art, New York (purchase).

a

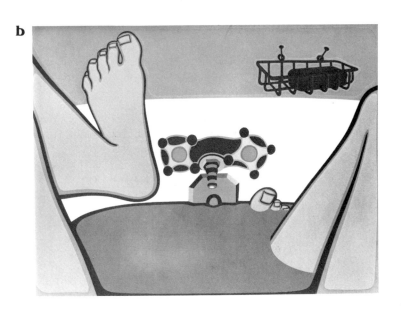

b

c

d

Illusion of Space

Recession

Plane/Diagonal Recession

In discussing pictorial space, one final concept must be mentioned. *How* does the recession into depth occur?

There are two basic devices. *Plane recession* shows distance by receding on a series of planes that are parallel to the picture plane. Recession is, therefore, slow and orderly; most of the movement is side-to-side or up-and-down. *Diagonal recession* is what the title implies. Planes are not flat, but recede diagonally on an angle, rapidly opening up the pictorial space. The movement is now back-and-forth or in-and-out. We are not discussing the degree of depth—how "deep" or "shallow" the picture is—but just *how* the recession is achieved.

In Mary Cassatt's etching **(a)**, the figures being mainly line are somewhat flat and create a horizontal plane in front of the flat wall and windows of the bus. In the distance a bridge makes another parallel plane. The plane recession is clear.

Canaletto's view of Venice **(b)** is entirely different. The emphasis here is on diagonals. The strong diagonal line created by the row of buildings recedes down the canal quickly, "pulling" us into a dramatic deep distance. Many of the gondolas reinforce this diagonal movement recession. The distance here may not be greater, but the feeling of depth is more dramatic.

White not trying for the illusion of great distance achieved in **b**, the painting by Edmund Tarbell **(c)** shows the same diagonal recession. Not one of the planes (walls, chairs, screen, door, etc.) is parallel to the picture plane. In addition, the man in the lower right corner, the woman, the door, and the far figure create a strong receding visual diagonal. This effect is more subtle than converging perspective lines, but the diagonal movement is equally clear.

While plane recession is less dramatic, it is not always dull or lifeless. The Matisse family portrait **(d)** clearly uses plane recession, and the painting does remain relatively flat, but the value contrasts and decorative patterns make a lively picture.

a Mary Cassatt. *In the Omnibus.* c. 1891. Drypoint and aquatint, 15 × 10½″ (37 × 27 cm). Museum of Art, Carnegie Institute, Pittsburgh, PA.
b Canaletto. *The Basin of St. Mark's, Venice.* 1735–41. Oil on canvas, 4 × 6′ (1.21 × 1.83 m). National Gallery, London (reproduced by courtesy of the Trustees).
c Edmund C. Tarbell. *The Breakfast Room.* 1896. Oil on canvas, 25 × 30″ (64 × 76 cm). Pennsylvania Academy of the Fine Arts, Philadelphia, PA.
d Henri Matisse. *The Painter's Family.* 1911. Oil on canvas. 4′8¼″ × 6′4⅜″ (1.43 × 1.94 m). Hermitage, Leningrad.

a

b

c

d

a

c

Spatial Puzzles

Illusion of Space

Artists all learn the various devices to give an illusion of depth or space. At times, certain artists purposely have ignored these conventions to provide an unexpected image. A confusion of spatial relationships is intriguing because the viewer is confronted with a visual puzzle rather than a statement.

Piranesi, in one of his many etchings of prisons **(a)**, not only ignores the "rules" but actually distorts them to create a wierd, spatially intricate scene. The confused, maze-like complexity of the enormous chamber serves as an ominous symbol of government bureaucracy and repression.

The English artist William Hogarth called his etching "a perspective joke" **(b)**. This humorous image contains all sorts of elements that destroy our initial impression of the scene. Absolutely impossible spatial things happen; and the more we look, the more nonsensical spatial incongruities we can find. The contemporary artist David Hockney has taken elements from this Hogarth etching for a work **(c)** that retains much of the original's spatial ambiguity.

Example **d** is a Surrealist painting. The whole thrust of Surrealism was to illustrate the impossible world of dreams and the subconscious mind. In **d** René Magritte gives us a truly strange painting. We are outside a building looking in a window, and the scene *inside* is another exterior. There is no way to explain this logically; we experience a strangeness.

The brilliance of M. C. Escher's draughtsmanship is shown in his lithograph *Waterfall* **(e)**. We cannot detect any mistakes in the perspective, yet an apparently straightforward scene suddenly becomes an impossible spatial situation.

a Giovanni Battista Piranesi. *The Prisons.* c. 1750. Etching, 21⅜ × 16¼" (54 × 41 cm). Metropolitan Museum of Art, New York (Harris Brisbane Dick Fund, 1937).
b William Hogarth. Frontispiece to Kirby's *Perspective.* 1754. Etching, 8¼ × 6¾" (21 × 17 cm). Metropolitan Museum of Art, New York (gift of Sarah Lazarus, 1891).
c David Hockney. *Kirby (After Hogarth) Useful Knowledge.* 1975. Oil on canvas, 6' × 5'⅛" (1.83 × 1.53 m). Museum of Modern Art, New York (gift of the artist and John Kasmin and Advisory Committee Fund).
d René Magritte. *In Praise of Dialectics.* 1937. Oil on canvas, 25⅛ × 21" (65 × 54 cm). National Gallery of Victoria, Melbourne, Australia (Felton Bequest, 1970).
e M. C. Escher. *Waterfall.* 1961. Lithograph, 14⅞ × 11¾" (38 × 30 cm). Escher Foundation, Gemeentemuseum, The Hague.

d

e

6

Rhythm

Introduction

Rhythm

Rhythm is a principle we associate with the sense of hearing. Without words, music can intrigue us by its pulsating beat, inducing us to tap a foot or perhaps dance. Poetry often has *meter,* which is a term for measurable rhythm. The pace of words can establish a cadence, a repetitive flow of syllables that makes reading poems aloud a pleasure. We also speak of the rhythm in movement displayed by athletes, dancers, and some workers performing manual tasks. And, of course, rhythm is a basic characteristic of nature. The successive pattern of the seasons, of day and night, of the tides, and even the movement of the planets in the universe—all exhibit a regular rhythm.

This same quality of rhythm can be applied to the visual arts, where the idea of rhythm is basically related to movement. Here the concept refers to the movement of the viewer's eye, a movement across recurrent motifs providing the repetition inherent in the idea of rhythm. Often in conversation we loosely apply the term "rhythmic" to any visual pattern that causes the eye to move quickly and easily from one element to another. But rhythm as a design principle is based on repetition. Repetition, as an element of visual unity, is exhibited in some manner by almost every work of art. However, rhythm involves a clear repetition of elements that are the same or only slightly modified.

While different in many respects, the two examples shown in **a** and **b** have the feeling of a similar visual rhythm. In both images a series of vertical elements extends across the design. The almost regular variations in light and dark provide a visual pattern of stress and pause, almost like the sound of a drum beating a rhythmic sequence.

The regularity of rhythm seen in **a** and **b** is not present in Kandinsky's painting (**c**). The eye again moves quickly through repeated circular elements, but the points of emphasis are now in a very irregular pattern. We are pushed and pulled in various directions, creating an exciting, unsettling rhythm.

---

a Gene Davis. *Billy Bud.* 1964. Acrylic on canvas, 5′8½″ × 6′4⅞″ (1.74 × 1.95 m). Charles Cowles Gallery, New York.

b Herbert Migdoll, designer, art director, and photographer. Souvenir program of *A Chorus Line,* four-page center foldout showing cast, published by New York Shakespeare Festival. American Institute of Graphic Arts, New York.

c Wassily Kandinsky. *Improvisation Sintflut.* 1913. Oil on canvas, 4′3⅜″ × 4′11″ (0.95 × 1.50 m). Städtische Galarie im Lenbachhaus, Munich.

c

Rhythm

Rhythm and Motion

We speak of the rhythmic repetition of colors or textures, but most often we think of rhythm in the context of shapes and their arrangement. Just as in music, some visual rhythms can be *legato*, or connecting and flowing; others are *staccato*, or abrupt and dynamic.

Our first impression of the watercolor in **a** is one of rapid movement. Our eye is jerked to the left by the heavy dark diagonal of the elevated railway. Within the design, repeated jagged triangular shapes are the dominant elements of the composition and establish an exciting rhythm of repeated shapes.

It is not just the free brushstroke of **a** that creates the dynamic rhythm. The painting in **b** achieves a similar effect with a very rigid, controlled technique. Painting **b** has small dark squares that move in a staccato pattern horizontally and vertically around the canvas. The recurrence of this motif establishes a visual rhythm. The irregular spacing of these small squares causes the pattern (and rhythm) to be lively, rather than monotonous. The artist, Piet Mondrian, titled this painting *Broadway Boogie-Woogie.* He has expressed in the most abstract visual terms not only the on/off patterns of Broadway's neon landscape but also the rhythmic sounds of 1940s instrumental blues music. The effect for us today is almost like the jumpy, always changing patterns we see in video games.

Contrast these examples with the photograph in **c**, where the feeling is very rhythmic, but flowing, sinuous, and very graceful. The rhythmic pattern an artist chooses very quickly establishes an emotional response in the viewer.

a John Marin. *Lower Manhattan.* 1920. Watercolor, 21⅞ × 26¾″ (56 × 68 cm). Museum of Modern Art, New York (Philip L. Goodwin Collection).

b Piet Mondrian. *Broadway Boogie-Woogie.* 1942–43. Oil on canvas, 4′2″ (1.27 m) square. Museum of Modern Art, New York (given anonymously).

c Albert Renger-Patzsch. *Trees.* 1936. Gelatin-silver print, 34 × 24″ (86 × 61 cm). Metropolitan Museum of Art, New York.

a

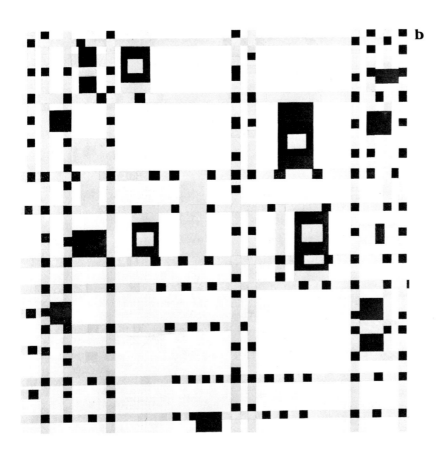

b

c

Alternating Rhythm

Rhythm

A special type of rhythm involves repetition in a slightly different way. When we look at a colonnaded Grecian temple **(a)**, with its repeating pattern of light columns and darker negative spaces, we say that the visual pattern is rhythmic. Here the design is an *alternating* rhythm—two motifs alternate with one another to produce a regular (and soon anticipated) sequence. This expected quality of the pattern is not a fault, for unless the repetition is fairly obvious, the whole idea of visual rhythm becomes obscure.

The repetitive effect of the knobby vertical linear elements in Jackson Pollock's *Blue Poles* **(b)** gives a similar rhythmic pattern, albeit a freer, less rigidly regular one. The main difference is that Pollock's intervening alternate areas are not simple negative spaces. Instead, these areas are filled with incredibly busy, complicated patterns of dribbled, spattered paint so typical of Pollock's work. If the vertical "poles" continued from top to bottom of the for-mat, they probably would function as negative, rather than positive, elements.

The same quality can be seen in **c**, a painting by Jacob Lawrence. In this work the tall, vertical, triangular shapes of the train seats move rhythmically across the painting, alternating with the abstracted, generally drooping, tired figures of the train's passengers.

a The Theseum (Hephaesteum), Athens. Begun 449 B.C.
b Jackson Pollock. *Blue Poles.* 1952. Mixed media, 6'11"½" × 16'1½" (2.12 × 4.89 m). Australian National Gallery, Canberra.
c Jacob Lawrence. *Going Home.* 1946. Gouache, 21½ × 29½" (55 × 75 cm). Collection IBM Corporation.

c

Rhythm

Progressive Rhythm

Another type of rhythm is called *progression,* or *progressive rhythm.* Again the rhythm involves repetition, but repetition of a shape that *changes* in a regular manner. There is a feeling of a sequential pattern. This type of rhythm is most often achieved with a progressive variation of the size of a shape, though its color, value, or texture could be the varying element. Progressive rhythm is extremely familiar to us; we experience it daily. Every time we look at buildings from an angle, the perspective changes the horizontals and verticals into a converging pattern that creates a regular sequence of shapes gradually diminishing in size.

The progression of concentric shapes in **a** establishes a rhythmic pattern. Radiating from the small black irregular square in the center, the shapes not only grow larger but subtly change to become more curvilinear and rounded as the size increases. All the brushstrokes repeat this same rhythmic pattern.

In **b** the rhythmic sequence of shapes moving horizontally across the format is clear whether we look at the white triangles or the black pointed planes. Both shapes progress regularly from narrow to wider and back again in an orderly rhythm.

Example **c** is similar to **a**, but here the increasingly larger circles are arranged in a freer, nonconcentric pattern. The rhythmic progression in size is still clear.

a Friedenreich Hundertwasser. *224 Der grosse Weg (The Big Road).* 1955. Mixed media, polyvinyl on canvas; 5′3⅛″ × 5′2⅜″ (1.62 × 1.6 m). Österreichische Galerie, Vienna. © Copyright 1983 by Gruener Janura AG, Glarus, Switzerland.

b Francis Celentano. *Flowing Phalanx.* 1965. Synthetic polymer on canvas, 34⅛ × 46⅛″ (87 × 117 cm). Museum of Modern Art, New York (Larry Aldrich Foundation Fund).

c Frantisek Kupka. *Disks of Newton.* 1912. Oil on canvas, 39½ × 29″ (101 × 74 cm). Philadelphia Museum of Art (Louise and Walter Arensberg Collection).

a

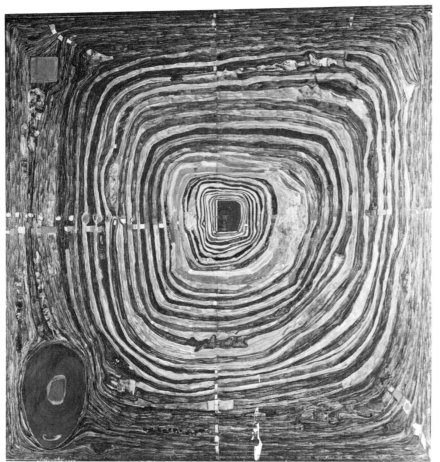

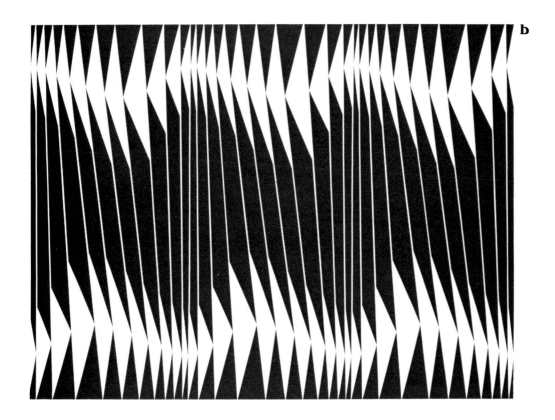

b

c

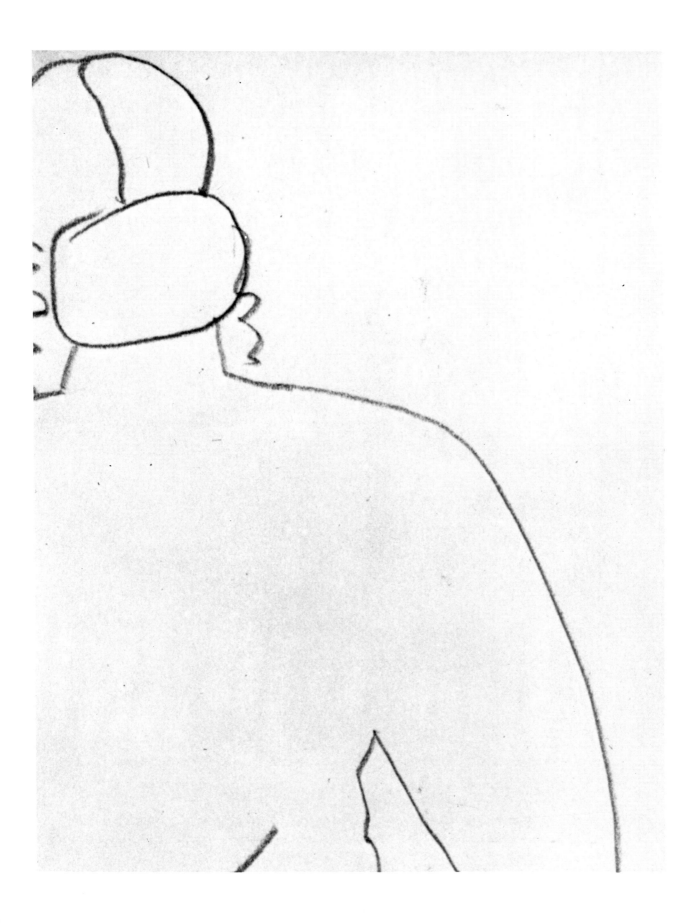

7

Line

a

b

Introduction

Line

Of all the elements in art, line is the most familiar to us. Since most of our writing and drawing tools are pointed, we have been making lines constantly since we were young children **(a)**.

What is a line? Other than a mark made by a pointed tool, it is a form that has length and width, but the width is so tiny compared to the length that we perceive the line as having only the latter dimension. Geometry defines a line as an infinite number of points. The usual art definition of a line is a moving dot. This latter definition is useful to remember because it recognizes the inherent dynamic quality of line. A line is created by movement. Since our eyes must move to follow it, a line's potential to suggest motion is basic. The impression of movement we feel when looking at the *Dancing Figure* **(b)** shows the idea clearly. The artist's line seems to be moving and "dancing" before our eyes. The rapid, dynamic quality of the line technique expresses the theme of the drawing.

Line is capable of infinite variety. Example **c** shows just a few of the almost unlimited variations possible in the category *line*. A curious feature of line is its power of suggestion. What an expressive tool it can be for the artist! A line is a minimum statement, made quickly with a minimum of effort, but seemingly able to convey all sorts of moods and feelings. The lines pictured in **c** are truly abstract shapes: they depict no objects. Yet we can read into them emotional and expressive qualities. Think of all the adjectives we can apply to lines. We often describe lines as being nervous, angry, happy, free, quiet, excited, calm, graceful, dancing*, and many other qualities. The power of suggestion of this basic element is very great.

a Mark Odom. Untitled drawing.
b Anonymous Italian. *Dancing Figure*. 16th century. Red chalk, 6¼ × 5¼" (16 × 13 cm). Metropolitan Museum of Art, New York (gift of Cornelius Vanderbilt, 1880).
c Line has almost unlimited variations.

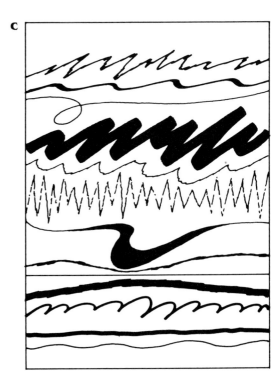

c

a

b

c

Line and Shape

Line

Line is important to the artist because it can describe shape, and by shape we recognize objects. Example **a** is immediately understood as a picture of an apple. It does not have the dimension or mass of an apple; it does not have the color or texture of an apple; it is not the actual size of an apple. Nevertheless, we recognize an apple from the one visual clue of its distinctive shape.

A cliché states that there are no lines in nature. This may be a bit misleading, since there *are* line-like elements in our natural and manufactured environment. Such things as tree twigs, telephone wires, spider webs, railroad tracks, and tall grass certainly are linear in feeling. What the cliché is addressing is illustrated in **b** and **c**. Example **c** is a line drawing—a drawing of *lines* that are *not* present in photograph **b** or in the original scene. In the photograph, of course, no black line runs around each object. The lines in drawing **c** actually show *edges,* while in the photo **(b)** areas of different value (or color) meet, showing the end of one object and the beginning of another. Line is, therefore, an artistic shorthand, useful because, with comparatively few strokes, an artist can describe and identify shapes so that we understand the image.

Line drawings, with the lines describing the edges of various forms, abound in art; **d** is just one example. The German artist George Grosz shows us a cafe crowded with drinkers. The many figures, tables, chairs, and plants are all described simply and quickly by nervous lines of the artist's pen.

a Line describes the shape of a form and helps us identify objects when other characteristics are missing.
b Areas of different value delineate the various objects in this scene.
c Line, as an artistic shorthand, depicts the edges of shapes.
d George Grosz. *Drinkers.* 1916. Pen and ink, 12⅞ × 8¼″ (33 × 21 cm). Fort Worth Art Museum, Tex.

d

Types of Line

Line has served artists as a basic tool ever since cave dwellers drew with charred sticks on the cave walls. *Actual* lines (**a**) may vary greatly in weight, character, and other qualities. Two other types of line also figure importantly in pictorial composition.

An *implied* line is created by positioning a series of points so that the eye tends automatically to connect them. The "dotted line" is an example familiar to us all (**b**). Think also of the "line" waiting for a bus; several figures standing in a row form an implied line.

A *psychic* line is illustrated in **c**. There is no real line, not even intermittent points; yet we *feel* a line, a mental connection between the two elements. This usually occurs when something looks or points in a certain direction. Our eyes invariably follow, and a psychic line results.

All three types of line are present in Perugino's painting of the Crucifixion (**d**). *Actual* lines are formed, for the edges of figures and background objects are clearly delineated. An *implied* line is created at the bottom, where the Virgin's feet, the base of the cross, and St. John's feet are points that connect into a horizontal line (**e**). This line is picked up in the horizontal shadows of the side panels. *Psychic* lines occur as our eyes follow the direction in which each figure is looking. St. John looks up at Christ, and Christ gazes down at the Virgin; this gives us a distinct feeling of a central triangle. Both St. Jerome and St. Mary Magdalene also look at Christ, forming a second, broader triangle. The purpose of these lines is to unify or visually tie together the various elements. Perugino's painting (**d**) may seem static, perhaps a bit posed and artificial, but it is admirably organized into a clear, coherent pattern.

Artists should always anticipate the movement of the viewer's eye around their compositions. To a large extent, they can control this movement, and the various types of lines can be a valuable tool.

a There are many types of actual lines, each varying in weight and character.
b The points in an implied line are automatically connected by the eye.
c When one object points to another, the eye connects the two in a psychic line.
d Pietro Perugino. *The Crucifixion with the Virgin, St. John, St. Jerome, and St. Mary Magdalene.* c. 1485. Oil on panel; center panel 39⅞ × 22¼" (101 × 57 cm), side panels 37½ × 12" (95 × 31 cm). National Gallery of Art, Washington, DC (Andrew W. Mellon Collection).
e Actual, implied, and psychic lines all are present in *The Crucifixion with the the Virgin, St. John, St. Jerome, and St. Mary Magdalene.*

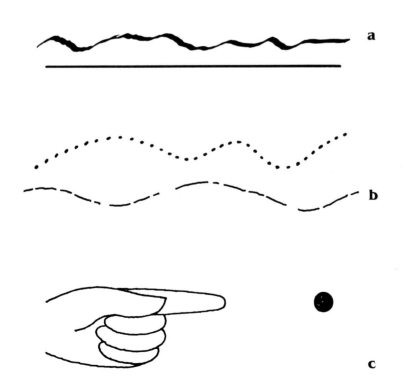

a

b

c

d

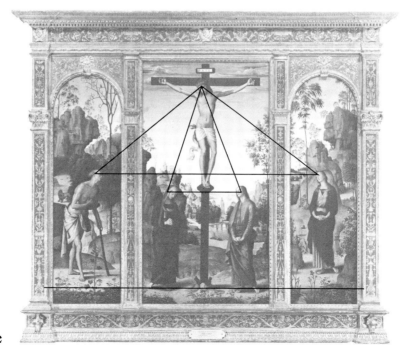

e

Line Direction

One important characteristic of line that should be remembered is its *direction*. A horizontal line implies quiet and repose, probably because we associate a horizontal body posture with rest or sleep. A vertical line, such as in a standing body, has more potential of activity. But the diagonal line most strongly suggests motion. In so many of the active movements of life (skiing, running, swinging, skating) the body is leaning, so we automatically see diagonals as indicating movement. There is no doubt that we imply more action, more dynamic momentum, from **b** than

from **a**. Example **a** is a static, calm pattern; **b** is exciting and changing.

One other factor is involved in the quality of direction. There are occasional round or oval paintings, but the vast majority of works are rectangular. Therefore, any horizontal or vertical line within the painting is parallel to, and repetitious of, an edge of the format. The horizontal and vertical lines within a design are called *stabilizers*, elements that reduce any feeling of movement. The lines in **a** are parallel to the top and bottom, but none of the lines in **b** are.

Poussin's painting **(c)** contains predominantly horizontal and vertical lines, with the diagonal road being the major exception. These lines are diagrammed in **d**. The emphasis, extending even to the clouds, is not just chance. The artist planned it. This painting often is called a *classical* work, a term that implies a static, serene, unchanging image. The emphasis on horizontals and verticals is a major factor in classicism.

Matisse's *Decorative Figure* **(e)** is an odd painting in respect to horizontals and verticals. We are accustomed to seeing pictures with figures in action posed against static backgrounds. Matisse has reversed this norm. The nude figure is highly rectilinear, with many horizontal and vertical outlines, and, therefore, quite immobile. The background fairly dances with diagonal lines, and writhing curves form diagonal patterns on the walls and floor.

a Horizontal lines usually imply rest or lack of motion.
b Diagonal lines usually imply movement and action.
c Nicolas Poussin. *The Funeral of Phocion*. 1648. Oil on canvas, 3′11″ × 5′10½″ (1.19 × 1.79 m). Louvre, Paris.
d The great number of horizontal and vertical lines in *The Funeral of Phocion* (**c**) suggest calmness and serenity.
e Henri Matisse. *Decorative Figure on an Ornamental Background*. 1927. Oil on canvas, c. 4 × 3′ (1.22 × .91 m). Musée National d'Art Moderne, Paris.

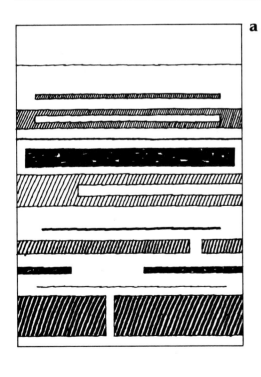

a

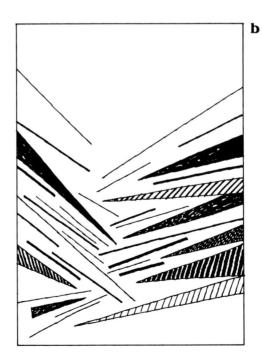

b

c

d

e

a

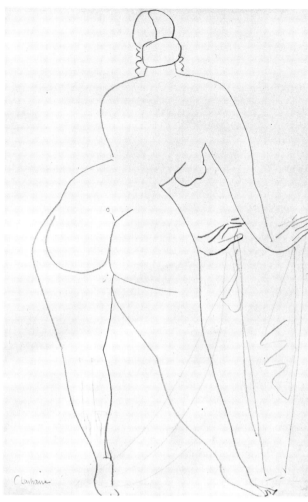

b

c

Contour and Gesture
Line

Regardless of the chosen medium, when line is the main element of an image, the result is called a *drawing*. There are two general types of drawings: *contour* and *gesture*.

When line is used to follow the edges of forms, to describe their outlines, the result is called a *contour* drawing. This is probably the most common use of line in art, and **a** is an example. This portrait by Ingres is a precise drawing with extremely delicate lines carefully describing the features and the folds of the coat. The slightly darker emphasis of the head establishes the focal point. We cannot help but admire the sureness of the drawing, the absolute accuracy of observation.

The drawing of a nude by Lachaise **(b)** is also a contour drawing, but this work has a markedly different character. It obviously was done very quickly, and the line moves rapidly and freely around the body's contours. Details are ignored; notice the sketchy quality of the hands and feet.

The artist's pencil suggests the voluptuous curves of the body in a spontaneous manner, rather than recording exact details.

The other common type of drawing is called a *gesture* drawing. In this instance, describing shapes is less important than showing the action taking place. Line does not stay at the edges, but moves freely within forms. Gesture drawings are not drawings of objects as much as drawings of movement. Because of its very nature, this type of drawing is almost always created quickly and spontaneously. It captures the momentary, changing aspect of the subject, rather than recording nuances

of form. Van Dyck's *Diana and Endymion* **(c)** is a gesture drawing. A few contour lines appear, but most lines are concerned with the movement of the swooping figures at the right and the swirl of drapery.

In the drawing by Diziani **(d)**, the rapid, almost scribbled ink line builds up the figures starting from the gesture of the poses, rather than beginning with clearly defined edges. The artist suggests swaying trees, but we see no definite foliage shapes.

While quite different approaches to drawing, these two categories of line are not mutually exclusive. Many drawings combine elements of both.

a Jean Auguste Dominique Ingres. *Portrait of a Young Man.* c. 1815. Pencil, 11½ × 8¾" (29 × 22 cm). Museum Boymans–van Beuningen, Rotterdam.
b Gaston Lachaise. *Standing Nude.* 1922–23. Pencil on paper, 17¾ × 11¾" (45 × 30 cm). Whitney Museum of American Art, New York (purchase).
c Anthony van Dyck. *Diana and Endymion.* 1621–30. Pen and brush, 7½ × 9" (19 × 23 cm). Pierpont Morgan Library, New York.
d Gaspare Diziani. *The Flight into Egypt.* 1733. Black pencil and pen and sepia on yellowish paper, 11⅝ × 8½" (30 × 22 cm). Museo Correr, Venice.

d

Line

Line Quality

To state that an artist uses line is not very descriptive because line is capable of infinite variety. The illustrations on these two pages give only a sampling of the linear possibilities available to the artist. A similar subject matter has been chosen so that differences in linear technique can be emphasized. The line technique chosen in each case is basically responsible for the different effects immediately obvious in the three works.

Example **a** shows a drawing by Ingres. Like many drawings, this was a study for a later painting, the *Grande Odalisque*. Artists often use the relatively easy and quick medium of drawing to try various compositional possibilities. Drawing **a** is an extremely elegant image. The sinuous, flowing curves of the nude are

rendered in a delicate, restrained, often almost disappearing, light line. The actual proportions of the body are altered to stress the long, sweeping, opposing curves that give the drawing its feeling of quiet grace.

The female nude by Marquet in **b** is not delicate in technique or feeling. Here the ink line, done with a brush, is heavy and bold, with variations of thickness. Rather than carefully rendering the body contours, Marquet merely suggests them with a spontaneous, dynamic line that moves quickly and somewhat imprecisely around the forms. The gray areas in the background, created with a nearly dry brush, reinforce the spontaneous effect, so that we can almost feel the rapid, scribble-like movement of the brush.

The drawing by Daumier **(c)** has a definite theme beyond portraying a woman: it is titled *Fright.* Notice how the line technique conveys this idea. The whole drawing implies movement; we can feel the woman pulling back, recoiling in fear. There is no one contour line. Many lines of varying weight and character (pencil and charcoal) evoke the forms. The hand, for example, is suggested with a few strokes, not clearly defined. Where the contour does emerge, it is built up of repeated strokes. Some lines are mere gesture lines showing the figure's movement. We can sense how the artist worked rapidly, moving quickly over the whole drawing.

The linear technique you choose can produce emotional or expressive qualities in the final pattern. Solid and bold, quiet and flowing, delicate and dainty, jagged and nervous, or countless other possibilities will influence the effect on the viewer of your drawing or design. Choose a theme or decide the effect you wish to impart, and fit the linear technique to it.

a Jean Auguste Dominique Ingres. Study for the *Grande Odalisque.* c. 1814. Pencil, 4⅞ × 10½" (12 × 27 cm). Louvre, Paris.

b Albert Marquet. *Nude.* c. 1910–12. Brush (?) and India ink, 11⅝ × 8⅛" (31 × 22 cm). National Gallery of Canada, Ottawa.

c Honoré Daumier. *Fright.* Pencil and charcoal, 8 × 9¼" (20 × 23 cm). Art Institute of Chicago (gift of Robert Allison).

a

b

c

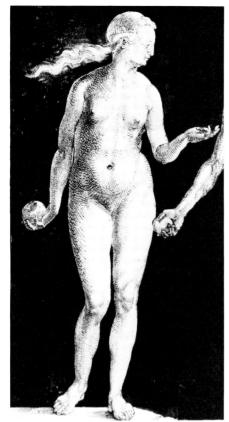

a

b

c

d

Line as Value

A single line can show the shape of objects. But an outlined shape is essentially flat; it does not suggest the volume of the original subject.

The artist can, by placing a series of lines close together, create visual areas of gray. By varying the number of lines and their proximity, an almost limitless number of "grays" can be produced. These resulting areas of dark and light (called areas of *value*) can begin to give the three-dimensional quality lacking in a pure contour line. Again, the specific linear technique and the quality of line can vary a great deal among different artists.

The pen-and-ink image of Eve (**a**)— a detail from Dürer's *Adam and Eve*— shows a strong contour edge because the light body contrasts with a stark brown background. Within the figure, Dürer then added a series of parallel lines in a criss-cross pattern (called *cross-hatching*) to create areas of gray, which give roundness to the figure. The pen produced nec-

essarily hard, definite strokes, which Dürer carefully controlled in direction to follow the volumes of the body forms.

The same pen-and-ink cross-hatching technique is clear in **b**. But in this illustration, the artist, Brad Holland, has used the lines in a looser manner, and the areas of gray are now more important and dominant than the outside contours.

Both **a** and **b** use line to carefully create naturalistic volumes and shapes. This effect is not so present in **c**. In Kirchner's portrait (**c**), the technique is very loose, more spontaneous, and even scribbled quickly in places. Kirchner's use of charcoal as the medium gives a linear effect

that is softer, more indistinct, and smudgy. The drawing emphasizes expression and feelings rather than a record of the visual image.

Ballerina, by Seurat (**d**), is a unique type of drawing. The line is almost totally confined to the background. The figure is silhouetted against areas of soft, vertical, linear strokes of conté crayon. Only a few lines within the body suggest the dancer's bodice straps, hat, and so forth. The effect is a soft, delicate understatement. Contour is vague and indefinite, with only a faint line here and there actually defining an edge, giving the drawing an abstract quality and a great contrast to the precise exactitude found in **a**.

a Albrecht Dürer. *Adam and Eve*, detail. 1504. Pen and broken ink with wash on white paper, entire work 9⅝ × 8" (24 × 20 cm). Pierpont Morgan Library, New York.
b Brad Holland. *The Observation Deck*. 1979. Ink, 8½ × 11" (22 × 28 cm). Courtesy the artist.
c Ernst Ludwig Kirchner. *Portrait of a Boy*. c. 1916. Charcoal, 23¼ × 19⅝" (59 × 50 cm). Kunsthalle, Hamburg. Copyright Dr. Wolfgang and Ingeborg Henze, Campione d'Italia, Switzerland.
d Georges Seurat. *Ballerina*. 1880 or 1884. Conté crayon, 9 × 5¾" (23 × 15 cm). Private collection, New York.

a

b

c

Line in Painting

Line *can* be an important element in painting. Since painting basically deals with areas of color, its effect is different from that of drawing, which limits the elements involved. Still, line becomes important to painting when the artist purposely chooses to outline forms, as Alice Neel does in her portrait **(a)**. Dark lines define the edges of the figure, the chair, and the large plant. The lines are bold and quite obvious.

Line can be seen in the detail of Venus from Botticelli's famous painting **(b)**. The goddess' hair is a beautiful pattern of flowing, graceful, swirling lines. The hand is delineated from the breast by only the slightest value difference; a dark, now quite delicate line clearly outlines the hand.

Compare the use of line in Botticelli's painting with that in **c**. Both works stress the use of line, but the similarity ends there. *Nurse*, by Roy Lichtenstein **(c)**, employs an extremely heavy, bold line—almost a crude line reminiscent of the drawing in comic books. Each artist has adapted his technique to his theme. Compare the treatment of the hair. Venus **(b)** is portrayed as the embodiment of all grace and beauty, her hair a mass of elegant lines in a delicate arabesque pattern. The nurse's hair **(c)**, by contrast, is a flat, colored area boldly outlined, with a few slashing, heavy strokes to define its texture. In a comment on North American culture, aesthetics and subtlety have been stripped away, leaving a crass, blatantly commercial image.

The use of a black or dark line in a design is often belittled as a "crutch." There is no doubt that a dark linear structure can often lend desirable emphasis when the initial color or value pattern seems to provide little excitement. Many artists, both past and present, have purposely chosen to exploit the decorative quality of dark line to enhance their work **(d)**.

a Alice Neel. *Nancy and the Rubber Plant.* 1975. Oil on canvas, 6'8" × 3' (2.03 × 0.91 m). Courtesy the artist.

b Sandro Botticelli. *The Birth of Venus*, detail. c. 1480. Oil on canvas, entire work 5'8⅞" × 9'1⅞" (1.75 × 2.79 m). Uffizi, Florence.

c Roy Lichtenstein. *Nurse.* 1964. Magna on canvas, 4' (1.22 m) square. Museum of Modern Art, Frankfurt.

d Henry Matisse. *The Pink Nude.* 1935. Oil on canvas, 26 × 36¼" (66 × 92 cm). Baltimore Museum of Art (Cone Collection).

d

Line in Painting

Line becomes important in a painting when the contours of the forms are sharply defined, and the viewer's eye is drawn to the edges. David's painting *The Death of Socrates* (**a**) contains no actual outlines, as we have seen in other examples. However, the contour edges of the many figures are very clearly defined. A clean edge separates each of the elements in the painting, so that a line tracing of these edges would show us the whole scene. The color adds interest, but we are most aware of the essential *drawing* underneath. As a mundane comparison, remember the coloring books we had as children and, as we took out our crayons, the parental warnings to "stay within the lines." Despite the absence of actual lines, the David work would be classified as a "linear" painting.

A linear painting is distinguished by its clarity. The emphasis on edges, with the resulting separation of forms, makes a clear, definite statement. Even an abstract painting, which simplifies form and ignores details, presents this effect (**b**).

One other facet of line's role in painting should be noted. Some artists use a linear technique in applying color. The color areas are built up by repeated linear strokes of the brush, which are not smoothed over. Toulouse-Lautrec's café scene (**c**) shows this technique. The artist actually drew with the brush; almost every area is constructed of variously colored linear strokes. The line direction varies to describe the different shapes.

Van Gogh used a similar technique in a more agitated, dynamic way (**d**). Short, linear strokes swirl around the painting. In both **c** and **d**, the multicolored lines give an interesting textural effect to the various areas and provide another element of visual unity.

a Jacques Louis David. *The Death of Socrates*. 1787. Oil on canvas, 4'3" × 6'5¼" (1.3 × 1.96 m). Metropolitan Museum of Art, New York (Wolfe Fund, 1931).
b Juan Gris. *Guitar and Flowers*. 1912. Oil on canvas, 44⅛ × 27⅝" (112 × 70 cm). Museum of Modern Art, New York (bequest of Anna Erickson Levene in memory of her husband, Dr. Phoebus Aaron Theodor Levene).
c Henri de Toulouse-Lautrec. *Monsieur Boileau at the Café*. 1893. Gouache on cardboard, 31½ × 25½" (80 × 65 cm). Cleveland Museum of Art (Hinman B. Hurlbut Collection).
d Vincent van Gogh. *Road with Cypresses*. 1890. Oil on canvas, 36 × 28½" (92 × 73 cm). Rijksmuseum Kröller-Müller, Otterlo, Netherlands.

a

b

c

d

 a

 b

 c

 d

Lost-and-Found Contour   Line

David's mythological work **(a)** is termed a *linear painting*. All of the forms are depicted with sharp, clear edges. There is no confusion about where one form ends and another begins. If we traced all of the contour edges **(b)**, we would have a line drawing that presents the entire scene. The color and value variations of the painting impart a feeling of volume and visual interest, but the line version is perfectly understandable.

The effect is quite different in **c**. This painting by de la Tour puts more emphasis on color and value than on line. In each of the figures, only part of the body is revealed by a sharp contour, but the edge then disappears into a mysterious darkness. This is termed *lost-and-found* contour: now you see it, now you don't. The artist gives us a few clues, and we fill in the rest. For example, when we see a sharply defined hand, we will automatically assume an arm is there, although we do not see it. A line interpretation **(d)** of this painting proves that we do not get a complete scene, but merely suggestions of form. Bits and pieces float, and it is more difficult to understand the image presented.

A strong linear contour structure in a painting provides clarity. Lost-and-found contour gives only relative clarity, for many forms are not fully described. However, the result is a more exciting emotional image.

The exciting effect of strong highlights and edges lost in darkness is, of course, not confined to painting. Artists in every medium use it. The photographer choosing the lighting for his subject often exploits the emotional effects of lost-and-found contour. Example **e** is just one of the countless photographs that have used the technique. Here a very beautiful and dramatic image has been produced from a simple architectural detail.

---

a Jacques Louis David. *Mars Disarmed by Venus and the Graces.* 1824. Oil on canvas, 9'10" × 8'7" (3 × 2.62 m). Musée Royal des Beaux-Arts, Brussels.

b The outlines of the forms in *Mars Disarmed* (**a**) are so clear that a line drawing of it is perfectly understandable.

c Georges de la Tour. *St. Sebastian Mourned by St. Irene and Her Ladies.* 1649. Oil on canvas, 5'3" × 4'3" (1.60 × 1.30 m). Staatliche Museen, West Berlin.

d A line drawing of *St. Sebastian* (**c**) is confusing because the shapes are defined by changing light and shadow, not by line.

e Mark Feldstein. *Untitled.* Photograph.

e

8

Shape/
Volume

Shape/Volume

Introduction

A *shape* is a visually perceived area created either by an enclosing line or by color and value changes defining the outer edges. A shape can also be called a *form*. The two terms are generally synonymous and often are used interchangeably. *Shape* is a more precise term because *form* has other meanings in art. For example, *form* may be used in a broad sense to describe the total visual organization of a work. A work's "artistic form" refers not just to shape but also to color, texture, value pattern, composition, and balance. Thus, to avoid confusion, the term *shape* is more specific.

Design, or composition, is basically the arrangement of shapes. The still life painted by 17th-century artist Judith Leyster **(a)** is an arrangement of various circular shapes varying in size. Of course, the color, texture, and value of these shapes are important, but the basic element is shape. Historically, line's most important role in art has been to delineate shape. Pictures certainly exist without color, without any significant textural interest, and even without line—but rarely without shape. Only the fuzziest, most diffuse of Impressionism's atmospheric images of light **(b)** can be said almost to dispense with shape.

In designing your own patterns and looking at others' patterns, you must develop the ability to look beyond interesting subject matter to the basic element of shape. The circles in **a** literally represent a basket, a glass, a jug, and various fruits. In another picture, the circle could be a wheel, the sun, an angel's halo, or some other round item. However, the circle's importance in pictorial composition is as a *shape.* In design, seeing shapes is primary; reading their meaning is interesting, but secondary.

Example **c** is a picture created by a computer. The image is interesting because it is clearly a pattern of some 250 squares of various grays *and,* incidentally, is a picture of Abraham Lincoln. In **c** a mid-point has been established at which we are aware equally of the basic design shapes and the subject matter. Several images were tested to find this mid-point, where most people could see both qualities. When more, smaller squares were used, people saw only LIncoln; with fewer, larger squares, they saw only the gray shapes and not Lincoln's head.

a Judith Leyster. *Still Life.* 17th century. Oil on canvas, 26¾ × 24⅜" (68 × 62 cm). Fine Arts Mutual, Inc., London.
b Claude Monet. *Morning Haze.* c. 1892. Oil on canvas, 29⅛ × 36⅝" (74 × 93 cm). National Gallery of Art, Washington, DC (Chester Dale Collection).
c Spatially quantized image of Abraham Lincoln. Blocpix® image. Courtesy E. T. Manning.

a

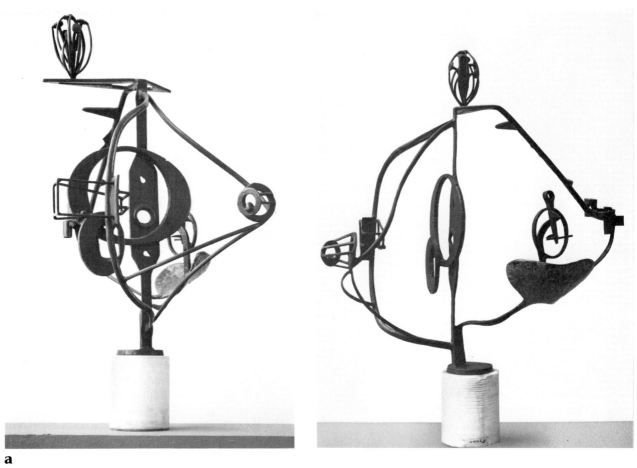

a

b

Volume/Mass

Shape/Volume

Shape usually is considered a two-dimensional element, and the word *volume* or *mass* is applied to the three-dimensional equivalent. In simplest terms, paintings have shapes, and sculptures have masses. The same terms and distinctions that are applied to shapes apply to three-dimensional volumes or masses. Although the two concepts are closely related, the design considerations of the artist can differ considerably when working in a two- or three-dimensional medium.

A flat work, such as a painting, can only be viewed satisfactorily from a limited number of angles and offers approximately the same image from each angle, but three-dimensional works can be viewed from countless angles as we move around them. The three-dimensional design changes each time we move; the forms are constantly seen in differing relationships. Unless we purposely stop and stare at a piece of sculpture, our visual experience is always fluid, not static. The two photographs of the piece of sculpture by David Smith (**a**) show how radically the design pattern can change depending on our angle of perception.

Thus, in composing art of three-dimensional volume or mass, the artist has more complex considerations. We may just step back to view the progress of our painting or drawing. With sculpture, we must view the work from a multitude of angles, anticipating all the viewpoints from which it may be seen.

Architecture is the art form most concerned with three-dimensional volumes. Unlike painting or drawing, architecture does not reproduce pictures or models of existing natural objects, but creates three-dimensional shapes by enclosing areas within walls. How often when we walk into a building we comment, "What a nice space." The created shapes are indeed empty *(negative)* spaces, but again many of the same design problems apply.

A sharp, clear-cut label for art as either two- or three-dimensional is not always possible. Relief sculptures *are* three-dimensional, but because the carving is relatively shallow with a flat back, they actually function more as paintings without color. And many contemporary artists now incorporate three-dimensional elements by attaching items to the canvas. To identify precisely as painting or sculpture such a work as the "installation" (**b**) by the American artist Jonathan Borofsky would be a problem.

a David Smith. *Blackburn: Song of an Irish Blacksmith,* front and side view. 1949–50. Steel and bronze, 46¼ × 41 × 24″ (117 × 104 × 61 cm); height of base 8″ (20 cm), diameter 7¼″ (18 cm). Wilhelm Lehmbruck Museum, Duisburg, Germany.

b Jonathan Borofsky. *Installation Paula Cooper Gallery.* 1980. Courtesy Paula Cooper Gallery, New York.

Shape/Volume

Naturalism and Distortion

The shapes in Eakins' portrait **(a)** would be described as *naturalistic.* The artist has skillfully reproduced the visual image, the forms, and proportions seen in nature, with an illusion of volume and three-dimensional space. Naturalism is what most people call "realism," meaning, of course, *visual* realism. The radically different visual effect of a similar subject in Soutine's painting **(b)** results from this artist's use of *distortion.* In using distortion, the artist disregards the shapes and forms of nature, purposely changing or exaggerating them. Sometimes distortion is meant to provoke an emotional response on the part of the viewer; sometimes it serves merely to emphasize the design elements inherent in the subject matter.

Many people think that distortion is a 20th-century development. Now that the camera can easily and cheaply reproduce the appearance of the world around us—a role formerly filled by painting—distortion or its degree has greatly increased in 20th-century art. However, distortion has always been a facet of art; the artist has rarely been just a human camera. Distortion of the figures is evident in the 11th-century illumination shown in **c**. We can identify distortion of size, of human proportions, and of anatomically possible positions. But in **d** the contemporary French sculptor Germaine Richier uses even greater distortion of human shapes and proportions. The grossly elongated forms and sharply acute angles of the limbs take on the attributes of the insect that the title suggests. The lumpy, uneven surface in **c** is a further distortion of the human body. This purposeful disregard of the naturalistic image achieves an emotional and quite menacing image.

a Thomas Eakins. *Miss Van Buren.* c. 1886–90. Oil on canvas, 44½ × 32″ (113 × 81 cm). Phillips Collection, Washington, DC.
b Chaim Soutine. *Woman in Red.* c. 1922. Oil on canvas, 25 × 21″ (64 × 53 cm). Musée d'Art Moderne de la Ville de Paris.
c *St. Matthew,* miniature from the Four Gospels. English, c. 1040. Manuscript illumination, 8⅛″ × 6¾″ (21 × 17 cm). Pierpont Morgan Library, New York.
d Germaine Richier. *Praying Mantis.* n.d. Bronze, height 4′5″ (1.35 m). Collection John Cowles, Minneapolis.

a

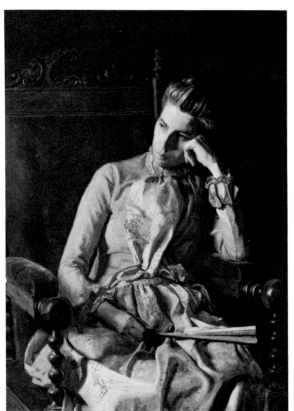

b

c

d

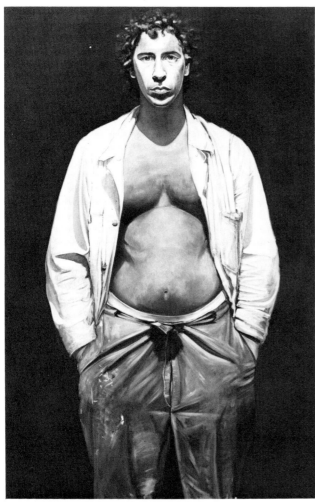

a

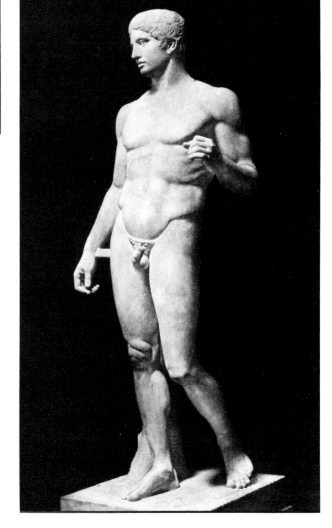

b

Naturalism and Idealism **Shape/Volume**

Naturalism is concerned with *appearance.* It gives the true-to-life, honest visual appearance of shapes in the world around us. In contrast, there is a specific type of artistic distortion called *idealism.* Idealism reproduces the world not as it is, but as it should be. Nature is improved upon. All the flaws, accidents, and incongruities of the visual world are corrected.

The self-portrait by Alfred Leslie **(a)** is naturalistic. Even in painting himself, the artist has indulged in no flattery. All the imperfections that affect the ordinary human body are presented in merciless detail. Every sag, bump, and bulge is faithfully recorded. The 5th-century B.C. statue **(b)** illustrates the opposite approach—idealism. This statue was a conscious attempt to discover the ideal proportions of the human body. No human figure was copied for this sculpture. The statue represents a visual paragon, a conceptual image of perfection that nature simply does not produce.

Idealism is a recurrent theme in art, as it is in civilized society. We are all idealistic; we all strive for perfection. Despite overwhelming historical evidence, we continue to believe we can create a world without war, poverty, sickness, or social injustice. Obviously, art will periodically reflect this dream of a utopia.

Today we are all familiar with a prevalent, if mundane, form of idealism. Large numbers of the advertisements we see daily are basically idealistic. Beautiful people in romantically lit, luxurious settings induce an atmosphere that is far different from the daily lives of most of us. But yet we *do* enjoy the glimpse of the "never-never land" awaiting if we use a certain product. Governments also often employ idealistic images to convince the world (or themselves) that their particular political system is superior. The heroic, triumphant figures in **c** are an example. Political propaganda is generally only naturalistic when portraying the opponent.

---

a Alfred Leslie. *Alfred Leslie.* 1966–67. Oil on canvas, 9 × 6′ (2.74 × 1.83 m). Whitney Museum of American Art, New York (gift of the Friends of the Whitney Museum of American Art).
b Polyclitus. *Spear Carrier.* Roman copy of Greek original of c. 450–440 B.C. Marble, height 6′6″ (1.98 m). Museo Nazionale, Naples.
c Vera Mukhina. *Machine Tractor Driver and Collective Farm Girl.* n.d. Sculpture. U.S.S.R. Economic Achievement Exhibition, Moscow.

c

a

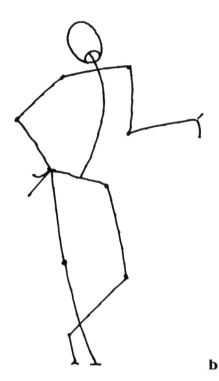

b

c

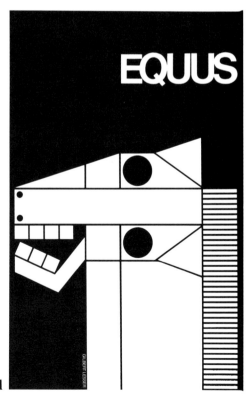

d

Abstraction

A specific kind of artistic distortion is called *abstraction*. Abstraction implies a simplification of natural shapes to their essential, basic character. Details are ignored as the shapes are reduced to their simplest terms. The stick figure that we all drew as children is a familiar (and extreme) example of abstraction. The Renaissance drawing of a man in **a** is *naturalistic* in recording all the complicated shapes comprising the human body. Example **b** conveys the same pose in the simplest way, ignoring every detail and reducing complex shapes to the few lines that define the figure's stance. These simple lines comprise the *essence* of the complicated structure in **a**.

Since no artist, no matter how skilled or careful, can possibly reproduce every detail of the natural scene, any painting could be called an abstraction. But the term most often is applied to works in which simplification is visually obvious and important to the final pictorial effect. Of course, the degree of abstraction can vary. In Grant Wood's painting

(**c**), almost all the elements have been abstracted to some extent. Many details have been omitted in reducing the hills to simple curving shapes and many of the trees to circular volumes. Still, the subject matter is immediately recognizable, and we are not too far from the naturalistic image. When the degree of abstraction is slight, as in this example, we often consider the shapes to be *generalized* or *stylized*.

In **d** the amount of abstraction is much greater. This poster for the play *Equus* clearly illustrates a horse's head, but the head has been highly simplified into a flat pattern of triangles, circles, and rectangles.

The horse's mane has become a series of parallel lines, and even the teeth are simple squares. This design illustrates the following widely accepted principle: all form, however complex, is essentially based on, and can be reduced to, a few geometric shapes.

Abstraction is not a new technique; artists have employed this device for centuries. If anything, the desire for naturalism in art is the more recent development. The Eskimo ceremonial carving in **e** clearly shows abstracted forms. Indeed, several of the carving's elements show a design similarity with the 20th-century poster in **d**.

a Antonio del Pollaiuolo. Study of *Adam*. Pen over black chalk with wash, 11 × 7¼″ (28 × 18 cm). Uffizi, Florence.
b An abstraction of the study of *Adam* (**a**) reveals its basic structure.
c Grant Wood. *Stone City*. 1930. Oil on board, 30¼ × 40″ (77 × 102 cm). Joslyn Art Museum, Omaha.
d Gilbert Lesser. Poster for the play *Equus*. 1976. Collage, 14 × 22″ (36 × 56 cm). Museum of Modern Art, New York (Permanent Design Collection).
e Mask of *Tunghâk, Keeper of the Game*. Inuit (south of the lower Yukon), 19th century. Painted wood, width 36¼″ (93 cm). National Museum of Natural History, Smithsonian Institution, Washington, DC.

e

Shape/Volume

Nonobjective Shapes

According to common usage, the term *abstraction* might be applied to the painting in **a**. This would be misleading, however, because the shapes in this work are not natural forms that have been artistically simpled. They do not represent anything other than the geometric forms we see. Rather, they are pure forms. A better term to describe these shapes is *nonobjective*—that is, shapes with no object reference and no subject-matter suggestion.

Most of the original design drawings in this book are nonobjective patterns. Often, it is easier to see an artistic principle or element without a distracting veneer of subject matter. In a similar way, artists in this century are forcing us to observe their works as visual patterns, not storytelling narratives. Without a story, subject, or even definable shapes, the painting must be appreciated solely as a visual design.

Lack of subject matter does not necessarily eliminate emotional content in the image. Some nonobjective works are cool, aloof, and unemotional. Paintings such as **a**

present purely nonobjective, geometric shapes that are, as Plato said, "free from the sting of desire." Example **b** is equally nonobjective, but the result is highly emotional. The thick paint in agitated, fluid brush strokes forms a dynamic pattern. This spontaneous, restless gesture painting is an exciting creation in pigment.

Whether any shape can be truly nonobjective is a good question. Can we really look at a circle just as a *circle* without beginning to think of some of the countless round objects in our environment? Artists often make use of this instinctive human reflex. A work such as Tony Smith's sculpture (**c**) appears to be a totally nonobjective pattern of forms, yet it reminds us of *some*thing. Reading the title *Gracehoper* immediately transforms the image into shapes reminiscent of a giant insect ("grasshopper"). Such reactions, even when not planned, are almost inevitable.

a László Moholy-Nagy. *A II*. 1924. Oil on canvas, 3′9⅝″ × 4′5⅝″ (1.16 × 1.36 m). Solomon R. Guggenheim Museum, New York.

b Willem de Kooning. *Park Rosenberg*. 1957. Oil on canvas, 6′8″ × 5′10½″ (2.03 × 1.79 m). Collection Mr. and Mrs. Donald Grossman, New York.

c Tony Smith. *Gracehoper*. 1972. Welded steel painted block, 23 × 22 × 46′ (7.01 × 6.71 × 14.02 m). Detroit Institute of Arts (Founders Society Purchase, donations from W. Hawkins Perry, Walter and Josephine Ford Fund, Eleanor Clay Ford, Marie and Alex Manoogian Funds and members of the Friends of Modern Art).

a

b

c

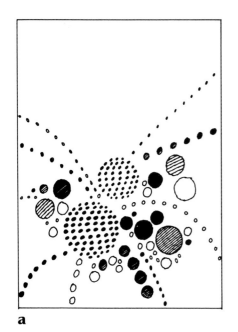

a

b

c

d

Dots

A *dot* is a shape, generally a very small one. The scale, however, is relative. What might be a "dot" in a large painting could be a large shape in a smaller drawing or print. It would be difficult to differentiate absolutely which of the shapes in **a** would qualify as a *dot* and which would not. As **a** illustrates, a dot can function in a design in three ways: (1) as a shape in itself; (2) in a sequential pattern that causes the eye to connect the points and create an implied line (a "dotted line"); (3) massed together to create a large shape—a shape that by its nature forms a gray value with interesting visual texture.

In massing dots to create areas of visual gray, we should recognize that most of the pictures reproduced in newspapers, magazines, and books are really collections of dots. Any black-and-white "halftone" (a picture with gradations of value) must be reproduced by photographing it through a *screen,* or grid. The screen translates the image into black dots

of different concentrations; when combined with the white paper, these dots give the visual effect of various grays. The gray tones in the humorous illustration **(b)** are also composed of dots, but these are created by the artist's pen, not mechanically by a screen.

Dots can be used either to create descriptive shapes or as pure design elements. The French artist Georges Seurat employed a technique called *pointillism,* in which the paint was applied in small dots of various colors **(c)**. The painted dots are com-

bined to create recognizable shapes. On the other hand, American artist Larry Poons uses dots just as dots **(d)**. He designs his paintings as mere compositions of "dots" in various colors and values. Poons's dots have no meaning and refer to no subject matter.

Dots may sometimes also be an element in three-dimensional design. A sculptural surface enlivened by mosaic tiles, or by discarded buttons and beads **(e)**, does become a pattern of "dots," which create lines and shapes.

a Dots can be used as individual design elements or as a part of larger shapes.
b Alex Murawski. *Jolly Green Giant.* 1978. Ink, 8⅝ × 12¾" (22 × 32 cm). Private collection.
c Georges Seurat. *The Channel at Gravelines, Petit Fort Philippe,* detail. 1890. Oil on canvas, 20 × 36¾" (74 × 93 cm). Indianapolis Museum of Art (gift of Mrs. James W. Fesler in memory of Daniel W. and Elizabeth C. Marmon).
d Larry Poons. *Away Out on the Mountain.* 1965. Acrylic on canvas, 6 × 12' (1.83 × 3.05 m). Allen Memorial Art Museum, Oberlin College, Oberlin, Ohio (Ruth C. Roush Fund for Contemporary Art).
e Larry Fuente. *Angel.* 1979. Sculpture created from various discarded materials, 6'8" high (2.03 m). Photographed by Louie Psihoyos.

e

Shape/Volume

Rectilinear and Curvilinear

The title of the painting by Theo van Doesburg (**a**) describes a theme of card players. However, the forms are so highly abstracted that the subject matter becomes relatively unimportant. What we see is a busy pattern of shapes that are all geometric in feeling—with hard, straight edges and angular corners. The term used to describe such shapes is *rectilinear*.

Aubrey Beardsley's drawing in **b** shows an equal emphasis on the opposite type of shape—*curvilinear*. All the forms in **b** are curving and twisting. The languid poses, the flowing drapery, the decorative accessories, and even the lavish wigs contribute to an incredibly intricate pattern of curvilinear shapes. This drawing is a product of a late 19th-century style called *Art Nouveau*, which put total pictorial emphasis on natural shapes.

We do think of curvilinear shapes as *natural*, reflecting the soft, flowing shapes found in nature. The term *biomorphic* is sometimes used to describe the same idea. Rectilinear shapes, being more regular and precise, suggest geometry and, hence, appear artificial and manufactured. Of course, these are very broad conclusions. In fact, geometric shapes abound in nature, especially in the microscopic structure of elements; and people design many objects with irregular, free-form shapes.

Illustrations **a** and **b** each concentrate exclusively on one type of shape. But most art combines both types. In using the two types of shapes, a useful device is to stress one type and use the other sparingly, as a point of emphasis. In the Gris painting (**c**), the table and wall panels make a rigid pattern of sharply defined rectilinear shapes, while the curves of the violin break the angular pattern and create a natural focal point.

Joan Miró's painting (**d**) also combines the two types of shapes. The artist has emphasized the curvilinear in the floating dark forms, while the background is divided into soft, slightly diffused rectangular forms.

a Theo van Doesburg. *Composition IX, Opus 18 (Card Players).* 1917. Oil on canvas, 45¼ × 41⅜″ (116 × 106 cm). Gemeentemuseum, The Hague.
b Aubrey Beardsley. *The Cave of Spleen.* n.d. Pen and ink, 9⅞ × 6⅞″ (25 × 17 cm). Museum of Fine Arts, Boston (Bigelow Collection, gift of the Estate of William Sturgis Bigelow).
c Juan Gris. *The Violin.* 1916. Oil on wood panel, 45½ × 28½″ (117 × 73 cm). Oeffentliche Kunstsammlung Basel, Basel.
d Joan Miró. *Painting.* 1933. Oil on canvas, 5′8½″ × 6′5¼″ (1.74 × 1.96 m). Museum of Modern Art, New York (gift of the Advisory Committee).

a

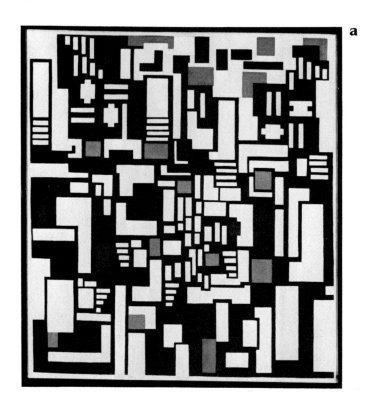

b

c

d

Shape/Volume

Positive/Negative Shapes

The four examples in **a** illustrate an important design consideration that is sometimes overlooked. In each of these patterns, the black shape is identical. The very different visual effects are caused solely by its placement within the format. This is because the location of the black shape immediately organizes the empty space into various shapes. We refer to these as *positive* and *negative* shapes. The black shape is a positive element, the white empty space the negative shape or shapes. *Figure* and *ground* are other terms used to describe the same idea—the black shape being the figure.

In paintings with subject matter, the distinction of object and background is usually clear. It is important to remember that *both* elements have been thoughtfully designed and planned by the artist. The subject is the focal point, but the negative areas created are equally important in the final pictorial effect. Japanese art often intrigues the Western viewer because of its unusual design of the negative spaces. In the Japanese print **(b)**, the unusual bend of the central figure and the flow of the robes to touch the edges of the picture create varied and interesting negative spaces. A more usual vertical pose for this figure would have formed more regular, symmetrical shapes in the negative areas.

Negative spaces need not be empty flat areas as painting **c**, by Mark Daily, illustrates. The areas surrounding the teapot and flowers have the same fluid brush strokes and value gradations that define the subject matter. This painting shows another, often unexpected, technique used by many artists. We would usually think of painting the "background" first, and then the foreground objects on top of it. But some artists reverse the procedure. Daily's painting **(c)** has many areas that show the negative area was painted *after* and on top of the positive.

The same positive/negative concept is applicable also to three-dimensional art forms. Architecture is, in essence, the enclosure of negative spaces. The sculpture of Henry Moore is noted for the careful integration of negative space "holes" within the composition. Even the utilitarian chair can be viewed as a design involving the two types of shapes. The tubular forms of Marcel Breuer's chair **(d)** enclose and define a series of negative voids that contrast with the solid areas of the seat, arms, and back.

a The location of shapes in space organizes the space into positive and negative areas.
b Tōshūsai Sharaku. *The Actor Segawa Tomisaburō as the Courtesan Tōyama Sheltering Ichikawa Kurizō as Higashiyama Yoshiwaka-Maru.* 1794. Woodcut, 13 × 5⅞″ (33 × 15 cm). Metropolitan Museum of Art, New York (Elisha Whittelsey Collection, Elisha Whittelsey Fund, 1949).
c Mark Daily. *Brooks Street Peonies.* 1976. Oil on canvas, 20 × 16″ (51 × 41 cm). Courtesy Sandra Wilson Galleries, Denver.
d Marcel Breuer. Armchair. 1925. Chrome-plated steel tube and canvas, height 28″ (71 cm). Manufactured by Gebrüder Thonet A. G., Germany. Museum of Modern Art, New York (gift of Herbert Bayer).

a

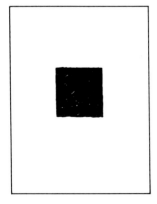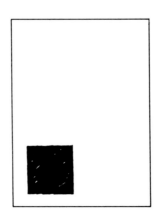

b

c

d

Shape/Volume

Positive/Negative Shapes

Integration

Design themes and purposes vary, but some integration between the positive and negative shapes is generally thought desirable. In **a** the shapes and their placement are interesting enough, but they seem to float aimlessly within the format. They also have what we call a "pasted-on" look, since there is little back-and-forth visual movement between the positive shapes and the negative white background. An unrelieved silhouette of every shape is usually not the most interesting spa-

tial solution. Example **b** shows the same shapes in the same positions as **a**, but the "background" is now broken into areas of value, which lend interest as well as better positive/negative integration. The division into positive and negative is flexible.

The integration of positive and negative shapes is so prevalent in art that innumerable works exhibit it. The most common device is to repeat a color in the positive and negative areas, giving them a visual link. The artist can also deliberately plan points where the eye will move from

object to background. In Botticelli's portrait (**c**), much of the figure is shown in silhouette. However, the darker window frame not only breaks the background into interesting areas but also provides several places where the figure and background are quite close in value, so that the viewer's eye moves easily from one to the other.

The background in the painting by Matisse (**d**) is broken into rather arbitrary areas of light and dark. These negative areas line up with, and continue the edges of, the positive shapes, but at the same time they contribute a visual variety: the positive elements are sometimes dark against light and at other times light against dark. Matisse's composition is a more sophisticated version of the effect created in **b**, and again the integration of the shapes is achieved.

a When positive and negative spaces are too rigidly defined, the result is rather uninteresting.
b If the negative areas are made more interesting, the positive-negative integration improves.
c Sandro Botticelli. *Portrait of a Young Man Holding a Trecento Medallion.* c. 1480. Oil on panel, 23 × 15½" (58 × 39 cm). Private Collection.
d Henri Matisse. *The Painter and His Model.* 1917. Oil on canvas, 4'9⅜" × 3'1⅞" (1.47 × 0.97 m). Musée National d'Art Moderne, Paris.

a

b

c

d

a

b

c

Positive/Negative Shapes

Shape/Volume

Confusion

Sometimes positive and negative shapes are integrated to such an extent that there is truly no visual distinction. When we look at the painting in **a**, we automatically see some black shapes on a background. But when we read the artist's title, *White Forms*, suddenly the view changes, and we begin to focus on the *white* shapes, with the black areas now perceived as negative space. The artist has purposely made the positive/negative relationship ambiguous.

Example **b** forces the same type of shift from dark to light in perception. Using shapes of numbers, instead of nonobjective brushstrokes, the designers have achieved the same positive/negative ambiguity in the simplest of patterns.

In most paintings of the past, the separation of object and background was easily seen, even if selected areas merged visually. But several 20th-century art styles literally do away with the distinction. The viewer's eye can no longer distinguish which shapes are positive and which negative—or perhaps the *whole* area now consists of positive shapes.

Futurism was an early 20th-century style that attempted to portray the moving, dynamic aspects of the modern world. Example **c**, a painting by the Futurist artist Gino Severini, is a pictorial expression of the constantly moving, shifting visual patterns seen in a Parisian nightclub. The surface of the painting shatters into fragmented images of the scene, suggesting constant movement and change. In the process, any sense of a background of nega-

tive shapes is lost, which perhaps is the artist's intent. The *Cubist* artists also created works that had little distinction between the positive and negative elements.

The works of M. C. Escher show the same intentional confusion of positive and negative shapes. With great imagination and brilliant technical facility, Escher creates designs that challenge the whole concept of a distinction between the two types of shape. Example **d** is one of many in which Escher literally abolishes negative space. No matter which color value we focus on in this remarkable design, the shapes appear as positive elements.

---

a Franz Kline. *White Forms.* 1955. Oil on canvas, 6'2⅜" × 4'2¼" (1.89 × 1.28 m). Museum of Modern Art, New York (gift of Philip Johnson).

b Chermayeff & Geismar Associates. "2,3". 1960. Letterpress printing, 9 × 12" (23 × 31 cm).

c Gino Severini. *Dynamic Hieroglyphic of the Bal Tabarin.* 1912. Oil on canvas with sequins, 5'3⅝" × 5'1½" (1.62 × 1.56 m). Museum of Modern Art, New York (acquired through the Lillie P. Bliss Bequest).

d M. C. Escher. *Study of Regular Division of the Plane with Horsemen.* 1946. India ink and watercolor, 12 × 9" (30 × 23 cm). Escher Foundation, Gemeentemuseum, The Hague.

d

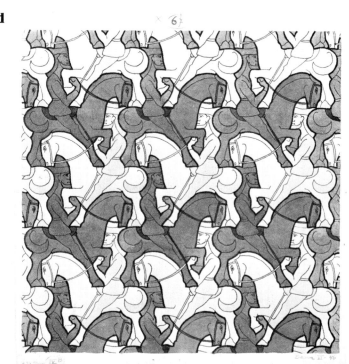

9

Texture

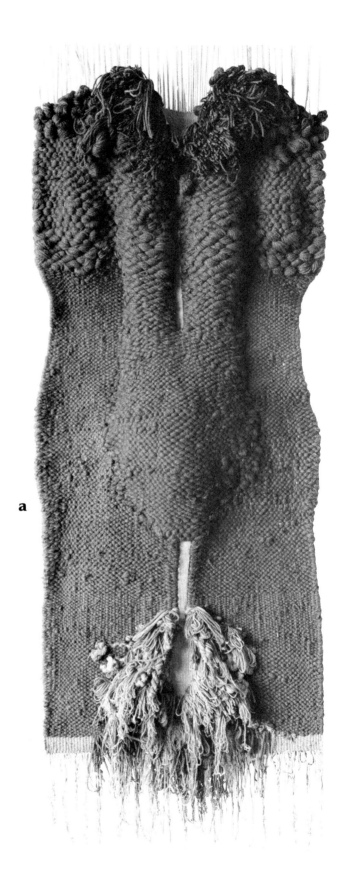

a

Introduction

Texture

Texture refers to the surface quality of objects. Texture appeals to our sense of touch. Even when we do not actually feel an object, our memory provides a sensory reaction or sensation of touch. In effect, the various light and dark patterns of different textures give visual clues for us to enjoy the textures vicariously. Of course, all objects have some surface quality, even if it is only an unrelieved smooth flatness. The element of texture is illustrated in art when an artist purposely exploits contrasts in surface to provide visual interest.

Many art forms have a basic concern with texture and its visual effects. In most of the craft areas, texture is an important consideration. Weaving and the textile arts **(a)**, ceramics, jewelry, and furniture design often rely heavily on the texture of the materials to enhance the design effect. The interior designer must be sensitive to the visual effects that textural contrasts can achieve.

Architecture today often relies on changes in texture for visual interest. Applied surface decoration has become less important; emphasis is placed on the honest look and "feel" of the materials. The design of the house in **b** uses simple rectangular forms in varying textures. The smooth sheen of glass is contrasted with warm, grained wood in flat horizontal and vertical ribbed patterns. Other areas gain further contrast from the rough, uneven texture of natural stone.

In sculpture exhibits, "Do Not Touch" signs are a practical (if unhappy) necessity, for so many sculptures appeal to our enjoyment of texture that we almost instinctively want to touch. The smooth translucence of marble, the rough grain of wood, the polish or patina of bronze, the irregular drop of molten solder—each adds a distinctive textural quality.

Visual distance can be a factor in texture. From a distance, many surfaces appear relatively smooth. The closer we get, the rougher and more varied the surface becomes, with microscopic photographs revealing textural patterns invisible to the naked eye.

a Grau-Garriga. *Vestal.* 1972. Tapestry of cotton, wool, and synthetics, 5'8" × 2'2" (1.7 × 0.65 m). Courtesy Arras Gallery, New York.
b Arthur Ericson. Private home, Vancouver, B.C.

b

Tactile Texture

There are two categories of artistic texture—*tactile* and *visual*. Architecture and sculpture employing actual materials have what is called *tactile* texture—texture that can actually be felt. In painting, the same term describes an uneven paint surface, when an artist uses thick pigment (a technique called *impasto*) so that a rough, three-dimensional paint surface results.

As the need and desire for illusionism in art faded, tactile texture became a more common aspect of painting. Paintings now could look like what they truly were—paint on canvas. Modifying the painting's surface became another option available to the artist. Van Gogh was an early exponent of the actual application of paint as a further expressive element. The detail in **a** shows how short brushstrokes of thick, undiluted paint are used to build up the agitated, swirling patterns of van Gogh's landscapes. The ridges and raised edges of the paint strokes are obvious to the viewer's eye.

The visual movement of painted strokes—often applied with a palette knife or very large brushes—was an important aspect of many Abstract Expressionist paintings. This technique resembled van Gogh's, but the result was even more dynamic because of the more spontaneous irregular strokes made by the artist. The tactile surface of a van Gogh may seem almost controlled and regular when compared to that of a de Kooning (**b**).

At times artists will even mix paint with other materials to add further tactile variety to the surface of the painting. The Spanish artist Antoni Tapies often combined thick pigment with plaster. Example **c** shows his *Great Painting*, a work of somber color but extremely rich tactile surface achieved partly by his mixing sand with the paint.

a Vincent van Gogh. *Road with Cypresses*, detail. 1890. Oil on canvas, entire work 36 × 28½″ (92 × 73 cm). Rijksmuseum Kröller-Müller, Otterlo, Netherlands.
b Willem de Kooning. *Woman, Sag Harbor*, detail. 1964. Oil on wood panel, entire work 6′8″ × 3′ (2.03 × 0.91 m). Hirshhorn Museum and Sculpture Garden, Smithsonian Institution, Washington, DC.
c Antoni Tapies. *Great Painting*. 1958. Oil and sand on canvas, 6′7″ × 8′6⅝″ (2.01 × 2.61 m). Solomon R. Guggenheim Museum, New York.

a

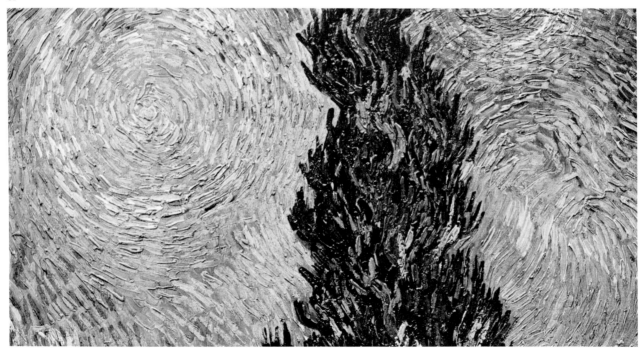

b

c

Tactile Texture

Collage

Creating a design by pasting down bits and pieces of colored and textured papers, cloth, or other materials is called *collage*. This artistic technique has been popular for centuries, but mainly in the area of folk art. Only in the 20th century has collage been seriously considered a legitimate medium of the fine arts.

The collage method is a very serviceable one. It saves the artist the painstaking, often tedious task of carefully reproducing textures in paint. Collage is an excellent medium for beginners. Forms can be altered or reshaped quickly and easily with scissors. Also, compositional arrangements can more easily be tested (before pasting) than when the design is indelibly rendered in paint.

The German artist Kurt Schwitters worked almost exclusively in collage. His *From Kate Steinitz* (a) is an arrangement of castoff scraps of colored and textured papers, with some areas of printed type creating further visual texture. In some places the paper is purposely wrinkled to add greater surface interest.

Anne Ryan, an American, worked mainly in collages of cloth. Her *Oval* (b) shows various bits of cloth of contrasting weaves and textures interspersed with bits of various papers. The value differences are so subtle that we concentrate on the tactile textures.

Working with old scraps of canvas and welded steel, Lee Bontecou created a textural relief that suggests a series of mouths (c). The inclusion of zippers in several of the open ovals suggests teeth and somehow gives a very frightening appearance to the whole collage.

---

a Kurt Schwitters. *From Kate Steinitz.* 1945. Collage, 13¼ × 10¼" (33 × 26 cm). Courtesy Marlborough Fine Art Ltd., London.
b Anne Ryan. *Oval.* n.d. Collage on paper, 6¾ × 5⅛" (16 × 21 cm). Private collection, United States.
c Lee Bontecou. *Untitled.* 1964. Welded steel with canvas, 6' × 6'10" × 1'6" (1.83 × 2.03 × 0.46 m). Honolulu Academy of Arts.

a

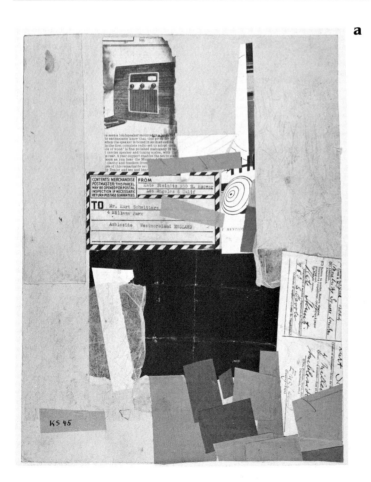

b

c

a

b

Visual Texture

In painting, artists can create the impression of texture on a flat, smooth paint surface. By reproducing the color and value patterns of familiar textures, painters can encourage us to see textures where none actually exist. This is called *visual* texture. The impression of texture is purely visual; it cannot be felt or enjoyed by touch; it is only suggested to our eyes.

One of the pleasures of still-life paintings is the contrast of visual textures. These works, lacking story or emotional content, can be purely visual delights as the artist plays one simulated texture against another. Still-life painting was extremely popular in 17th-century Flemish art, and countless beautiful examples were created. Portraits such as the one by van Dyck in **a** are interesting today not because of the largely unknown sitter, but because of the rendition of visual textures. The artist has so skillfully suggested the sheen of the satin sleeves, the delicacy of the lace collar, the incredibly fluffy feather fan, and much more.

The *Surrealist* artist Max Ernst uses visual texture to help create the eerie mood of his painting *The Eye of Silence* (**b**). A dank, stagnant pool is surrounded by rocks and ruins, all encrusted with creeping, decaying vegetation. The convincing rendering of these textures gives the picture its weird, frightening atmosphere.

The building in **c** is in a different medium and wildly different scale, yet shares the tradition of examples **a** and **b**. The blank, lifeless side wall of the building has been transformed by a startling painting. A painted brick wall is apparently opened by a giant zipper to reveal a neoclassical building behind it. A wonderfully absurd image results. Visual texture is clearly not confined to small-scale, still-life painting.

a Anthony van Dyck. *Marie-Louise de Tassis*. c. 1630. Oil on canvas. 4′3⅛″ × 3′1″ (1.30 × 0.94 m). Collection of the reigning Count of Lichtenstein, Schloss-Vaduz.
b Max Ernst. *The Eye of Silence*. 1943–44. Oil on canvas, 3′6½″ × 4′7½″ (1.08 × 1.41 m). Washington University Gallery of Art, St. Louis, MO.
c Gert Neuhaus. Street mural, Zillestrasse, Berlin. 1979. Photographed by Volker Barthelmeh.

c

a

b

c

Visual Texture

Trompe-l'oeil

The ultimate point in portraying visual texture is called *trompe-l'oeil*, the French term meaning "to fool the eye." This style is commonly defined as "deceptive painting." In trompe-l'oeil the objects, in sharp focus, are delineated with meticulous care. The artist copies the exact visual color and value pattern of each surface. A deception occurs because the appearance of objects is so skillfully reproduced that we are momentarily fooled. We look closer, even though our rational brain identifies the image as a painting and not the actual object.

William Harnett, a 19th-century American artist, was a well-known practitioner of trompe-l'oeil painting. Example **a** is especially confusing. A lithographic reproduction of Harnett's famous painting *The Old Violin* has been framed in wood with actual hinges and hardware continuing the painted forms. Separating reality and illusion becomes an entertaining problem for the viewer.

Example **b** illustrates an amusing extension of the illusion. Here the carefully rendered papers are covered by a piece of broken "glass," which proves to be merely painted also.

But careful painted rendering to simulate textures is not limited to art of the past. Interest in trompe-l'oeil has revived, along with the general trend back to naturalism in contemporary art.

Even in sculpture the trompe-l'oeil tradition is alive. The incredibly realistic *Golf Bag* by Marilyn Levine **(c)** is actually made of ceramic, but until one touches or attempts to lift it, the illusion is superb.

The revived interest in naturalism, as a reaction to the abstractions and distortions of the mid-century, has resulted in movements such as *Super-Realism*. Illustration **d** reproduces a painting in acrylics, not a photograph. It would be easy to be fooled, however, as every detail is presented with photo-like naturalism. The subject is drawn with technical precision and rendered with absolute clarity and exactitude. We may not be fooled into thinking we are seeing the actual scene, but we would not immediately think that **d** is a painting.

a William Harnett. *The Old Violin.* 1886. Lithographic reproduction by Gus Ilg, 1887, with frame in three dimensions; 42¾ × 31¾" (109 × 81 cm). Philadelphia Museum of Art (given by Dr. John O'Neill).
b Laurent Dabos. *Peace Treaty Between France and Spain.* Oil on canvas, 23 × 18" (59 × 46 cm). Musée Marmottan, Paris.
c Marilyn Levine. *Golf Bag.* 1976. Ceramic, on wooden board; 35½ × 13 × 6" (90 × 33 × 15 cm). Collection Monroe R. and Leila Meyerson.
d Franz Gertsch. *Making Up.* 1975. Acrylic on canvas, 7'8" × 11'4¼" (2.34 × 3.47 m). Museum Ludwig, Cologne.

d

Texture

Texture and Pattern

It would be difficult to draw a strict line between *texture* and *pattern*. We immediately associate the word *pattern* with printed fabrics such as plaids, stripes, polka dots, and floral "patterns" **(a)**. *Pattern* is usually defined as a repetitive design, with the same motif appearing again and again. Texture, too, often repeats, but its variations do not involve such perfect regularity. The difference in the two terms is often slight. A material such as burlap would readily be identified as a tactile texture, yet the surface is repetitive enough to be called a pattern.

The essential distinction between texture and pattern seems to be whether the surface arouses our sense of touch or merely provides designs appealing to the eye. While not mechanically repetitive, the designs dominating the portrait by Klimt in **b** would clearly be called pattern, not texture. They do not appeal to our sense of touch, but create decorative colored figures—literally surface patterns. The naturalistically rendered body emerging from the ornate, flat, patterned surface provides a startling contrast.

The interlocking jigsaw-puzzle shapes of Dubuffet's painting **(c)** produce a busy design of contrasting patterns, not textures.

a Printed patterns often serve as decorative elements in interior design.

b Gustave Klimt. *Adele Bloch-Bauer.* 1907. Oil on canvas, 44⅝" (140 cm) square. Österreichische Galerie, Vienna. Copyright by Galerie Welz, Salzburg.

c Jean Dubuffet. *Nimble Free Hand (Mouchon Berloque).* 1964. Acrylic on canvas, 4'11" × 6'7" (1.5 × 2.01 m). Tate Gallery, London.

a

10

Color/Value

Color/Value

Introduction

Value and *color* are two terms that are closely related

Value is simply the artistic term for light and dark; an area's value is its relative lightness or darkness in a given context. Only through changes of light and dark can we perceive anything. Light reveals forms; in a dark room at night we *see* nothing and bump into furniture and walls. The page you are reading now is legible only because the darkness of the type contrasts with the whiteness of the background paper. Even the person (or animal) who is physiologically unable to perceive color can function with only minimal difficulties by perception based on varying tones of gray.

Example **a** is a scale of seven values of grays. These are termed *achromatic* grays, as they are mixtures of only black and white: no color (or chroma) is used. While this scale shows only seven steps, the average eye is able to discern around forty variations in value.

The term *value contrast* refers to the relationship between areas of dark and light. Because the scale in **a** is arranged in sequential order, the contrast between any two adjoining areas is rather slight and termed *low-value* contrast. The center gray circles, which are a constant middle value, show higher value contrast at the top and bottom of the scale than toward the middle.

Color, based on wave-lengths of light, offers a much broader field of visual differences and contrasts. But grayed neutrals (now called *chromatic* grays) can also be produced by mixing certain colors, which result in different tones than those in **a**. A further relationship of value and color is that every color is, in itself, also simultaneously a certain value. Pure yellow is a light (high-value) color corresponding to a very light gray in terms of light reflection. Purple is basically a dark, low-value color that would match a very dark gray.

When we look at **b**, we are intrigued by the pattern of various colors, since subject matter is absent. The whole creative premise of Vasarely's serigraph is based on color and the relationship of hues and the spatial effects of color. In **c** the same work is shown only in all the corresponding tones of gray. The result is not as effective, yet the basic structure is still clear. The pattern and visual rhythm of the original is interesting even devoid of color. Notice that in both **b** and **c** some of the circles pop forward and command our attention because of the strong dark and light contrast with their backgrounds; other areas of less value contrast become subordinate. Color adds an important dimension and stimulating interest, but value alone can provide an understandable and satisfying image.

a A value scale of gray. The center gray circles are identical in value.
b Victor Vasarely. *Untitled,* Plate 2 from the portfolio *Planetary Folklore.* 1964. Color screenprint, 24¾ × 23⅜″ (63 × 59 cm). Museum of Modern Art, New York (Larry Aldrich Fund).
c Victor Vasarely. *Untitled,* Plate 2 from the portfolio *Planetary Folklore.* 1964. Color screenprint, 24¾ × 23⅜″ (63 × 59 cm). Museum of Modern Art, New York (Larry Aldrich Fund).

a

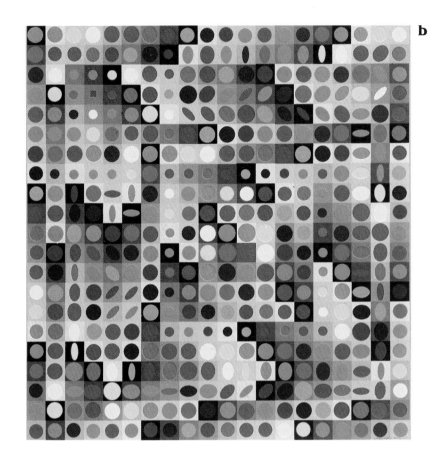

b

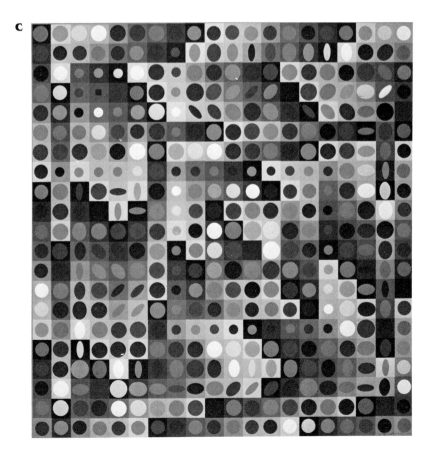

c

Value Pattern

In describing paintings or designs, we often speak of their *value pattern.* This term refers to the arrangement and the amount of variation in light and dark, independent of the colors used.

When value contrast is minimized and all the values are within a limited range with only small variation, the result is a restrained, subtle effect. The impression is one of understatement, whether the value range is limited to lights (*high* key is a term often used) or darks (*low* key). In Richard Dadd's watercolor **(a)**, the values are all extremely light with really no contrasting dark areas, just a few slightly darker lines here and there. The painting in **b** shows the opposite approach, an extreme contrast of dark and light. This is a Baroque painting, done in a period when artists purposely accentuated value contrasts to portray exciting themes. This use of highly contrasting values is called *Tenebrism.* The violent and gory subject of Artemisia Gentileschi's painting **(b)** receives an aptly emotional visual treatment. The light from the single candle casts dramatic, sudden shadows throughout the scene, achieving almost a theatrical effect.

Our different responses to **a** and **b** illustrate how value alone can create an immediate emotional reaction. The artist can choose a value pattern to elicit emotional reactions in the viewer. Closely related values are calm and quiet. The theme of the harem in **a** is shown with unnaturally light values, and the shapes are barely discernable. An exotic, mystical, almost magical mood results. On the other hand, sharp value contrasts suggest drama, excitement, even conflict. Certainly, the gruesome theme of **b** would not be communicated by the limited range of values in **a**. An entirely different mood would have been presented.

In the same way, overall darkness may provide feelings of sadness, depression, and even mystery. Lighter values, being brighter, seem less serious or threatening. Specific colors will always evoke emotional reactions, but the value pattern alone can be important in expressing a theme.

The painting in **b** shows values that could be seen in a candlelit room. In drawing **c**, by Aubrey Beardsley, the value pattern does not refer to any specific light source, but is used in a more decorative and abstract (though no less emotional) manner. This drawing with its overall, pervading black seems ominous. The sharply contrasting white highlights on the main figure's tiny, distorted, crabbed face and on her large, lustful, bared breasts immediately suggest evil. We need know nothing of the Roman empress Messalina to see **c** as a menacing picture of corruption and sin. The values chosen complement the emotional content of the drawn forms.

a Richard Dadd. *Fantasie de l'Harem Égyptien.* 1865. Watercolor, $10\frac{7}{8} \times 7''$ (48×18 cm). Ashmolean Museum, Oxford.

b Artemisia Gentileschi. *Judith and Maidservant with the Head of Holofernes.* c. 1625. Oil on canvas, $6'\frac{1}{2}'' \times 4'7\frac{3}{4}''$ (1.84×1.42 m). Detroit Institute of Arts (gift of Mr. Leslie H. Green).

c Aubrey Beardsley. *Messalina and Her Companion,* illustration for the sixth satire of Juvenal. 1895. Pencil, india ink, and watercolor, $11 \times 7''$ (28×18 cm). Tate Gallery, London.

a

b

Value as Emphasis

Color/Value

A valuable use of dark and light contrast is to create a focal point or center of attention in a design. A visual emphasis or "starting point" is often desired. A thematically important character or feature can be visually emphasized by value contrast. High dark and light contrast instantly attracts our attention. So by planning high contrast in one area and subdued contrast elsewhere, the artist can be assured where the viewer's eye will be directed first.

The focal point in Gustave Moreau's painting (**a**) is immediately established by value. Almost the entire painting is done in closely related very dark values. The dancing figure of Salome is then accentuated by her sudden, much lighter value. She appears almost as if in a spotlight on a darkened stage.

Moreau's use of value is very effective, it not overly subtle. The painting by Hopper (**b**) uses the same technique in a less obvious way. The sharp white of the interior of the brightly lit cafe contrasts with the general darkness outside. This light then "frames" the several dark figures, who become the focal point of the painting. The general isolation of these dark spots reinforces the quiet, almost melancholy mood of the painting.

Paintings **a** and **b** are, of course, done in color. But the black-and-white reproductions here are valuable to show the artists' reliance on value contrast, irrespective of the particular colors involved. Most artists are as aware of the value pattern they create as of the pattern of various colors. The artistic choice is often not "green" or "red," but how dark (or light) a green or red to use.

When value contrast is evenly distributed throughout a design, the result is usually a work with overall emphasis and no clear visual importance of any one part. This is sometimes a conscious choice of the artist, but somewhat rare. The early Cubist painters stressed value rather than color differences, often with quite limited contrast. The analysis and abstraction of form was paramount in Cubist patterns of innumerable planes in almost one hue and only subtle changes in dark and light. But while the values in the Picasso portrait (**c**) are closely related, the very slightly higher contrast around the head still establishes a focal point.

a Gustave Moreau. *Salome Dancing Before Herod.* 1876. Oil on canvas, 36½ × 24" (93 × 61 cm). Musée Gustave Moreau, Paris.
b Edward Hopper. *Nighthawks.* 1942. Oil on canvas, 2'6" × 5' (0.76 × 1.52 m). Art Institute of Chicago.
c Pablo Picasso. *Daniel Henry Kahnweiler.* 1910. Oil on canvas, 39⅝ × 28⅝" (101 × 73 cm). Art Institute of Chicago (gift of Mrs. Gilbert W. Chapman).

c

Color/Value

Value and Space

One of the most important uses of gradations of dark and light is to suggest volume or space.

On a flat surface, value can be used to impart a three-dimensional quality to shapes. During the Renaissance, the word *chiarscuro* was coined to describe the artistic device of implying depth and volume in a painting or drawing. *Chiarscuro* is a combination of the Italian words for "light" and "dark." A drawing using only line **(a)** is very effective in showing shapes. By varying the weight of the line, an artist may imply dimension or solidity, but the effect is subtle. When areas of dark and light are added **(b)**, we begin to feel the three-dimensional quality of forms. And as all photographers soon learn, the light direction is important: front lighting flattens form, side lighting emphasizes volume, back or below lighting can distort form into unexpected patterns used for design or emotional reasons.

Along the same idea, another aspect of value's ability to suggest depth is important. Much art has been, and is, concerned with producing a simulation of our three-dimensional world. On a two-dimensional piece of paper or canvas, an *illusion* of space is desired—and perhaps not just the roundness of a head or apple, but a whole scene receding far into the distance. Here again the use of value can be a valuable tool of the artist. High-value contrast seems to come forward, to be actually *closer,* while areas of lesser contrast recede or stay back, suggesting distance. Notice how effectively Caspar Friedrich has used this technique in painting **c**. The figure on the rocks in front is sharply dark against the rest of the picture. Then each receding rock, wave, and bit of land becomes progressively lighter and closer to the value of the sky. An illusion of great depth is thus created by manipulating the various values.

This technique does reproduce what our eyes see: far-off images visually become grayer and less distinct as the distance increases. In art, this is called *aerial,* or *atmospheric,* perspective.

a John Frazer. *Self-Portrait.* 1959. Pen and ink. Collection Yale University Art Gallery, New Haven, CT.

b Pierre-Paul Prud'hon. *Head of Vengeance,* study for *Justice and Vengeance Pursuing Crime.* 1808. Black and white chalk and estompe on blue paper, 20 × 15½" (51 × 39 cm). Art Institute of Chicago (Arthur Heun Fund).

c Caspar David Friedrich. *The Wanderer Above the Sea of Mist.* c. 1817–18. Oil on canvas, 38⅜ × 29¼" (99 × 75 cm). Kunsthalle, Hamburg.

a

b

c

Color/Value

Color Characteristics

Color has a basic, instinctive visual appeal. Great art has been created in black and white, but few artists have totally ignored the added visual interest that color lends. The uninhibited use of color has been a primary characteristic of art in this century. Indeed, our world today is marked by bold uses of color in every area of ordinary living. We are confronted now with color choices in all kinds of new areas. Everything—from home appliances to bank checks—has blossomed out in bright colors. Fashion design, interior design, architecture, industrial design—all areas of art are now increasingly concerned with color.

Every artist or art student must be concerned with a study of color to some extent. Today's artists and students (and authors) owe a great debt to the contemporary American artist Josef Albers, who as painter and teacher has devoted a career to the study of color and color relationships. His books and paintings have contributed invaluably to our knowledge of color. Many of the concepts in this discussion are reflections of his research and teaching.

Color theory is an extremely complex science. A thorough study of such factors as the various light wave-lengths of different colors or the color/heat relationship is interesting but complicated, and goes beyond our concern here.

For artists, the essential fact of color theory is that color is a property of *light*, not an object itself. This property of light was illustrated by Sir Isaac Newton in the 17th century, when he put white light through a prism (**a**). The prism broke up white light into the familiar rainbow of hues. Objects have no color of their own, but merely have the ability to reflect certain rays of white light, which contains all the colors. Blue objects absorb all the rays except the blue ones, and these are reflected to our eyes. Black objects *absorb* all the rays; white objects *reflect* all of them. The significance of this fact for the artist is that as light changes, color will change. What color is grass? Green? Grass may be almost gray at dawn, bright green at noon, and nearly black at midnight. There is no one consistent color for any thing or object.

Related to this same idea, one other color phenomenon is important: colors change according to their surroundings. Even in the same light, a color will appear different depending on the colors that are adjacent to it. Rarely do we see a color by itself. Perhaps an occasional room or a certain stage set presents just one color, but this is unusual. Normally, colors are seen in conjunction with others, and the visual differences are often amazing. A change in value (dark and light) is a common occurrence. Example **b** illustrates that even the color effect itself changes. The smaller red-purple squares are identical; the visual differences are caused by the various background colors these squares are placed against.

The phenomenon of color change is another variable. In working with color, you will soon discover that some colors are more susceptible to change than others. In looking at **b**, it is hard to believe the four pink squares are the identical color. In **c**, however, the two yellow areas, despite different backgrounds, still look about the same. With pure, vibrant colors, optical changes will be very slight. Grayed, neutral colors (called *broken* colors) are constantly changing in different contexts.

a A ray of white light projected through a prism separates into the hues seen in a rainbow.
b The red-purple squares, although seemingly different, are identical.
c A brilliant, vibrant color will not show much change despite different surroundings.

a

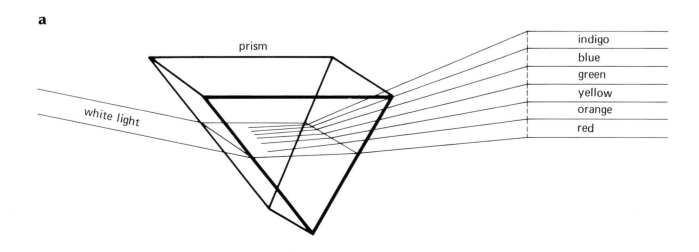

prism

white light

indigo
blue
green
yellow
orange
red

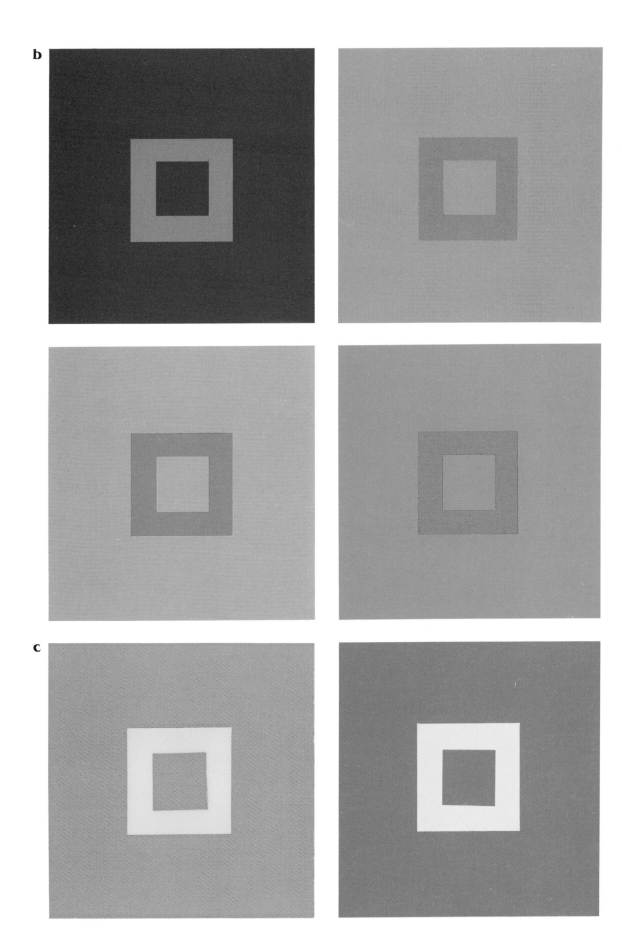

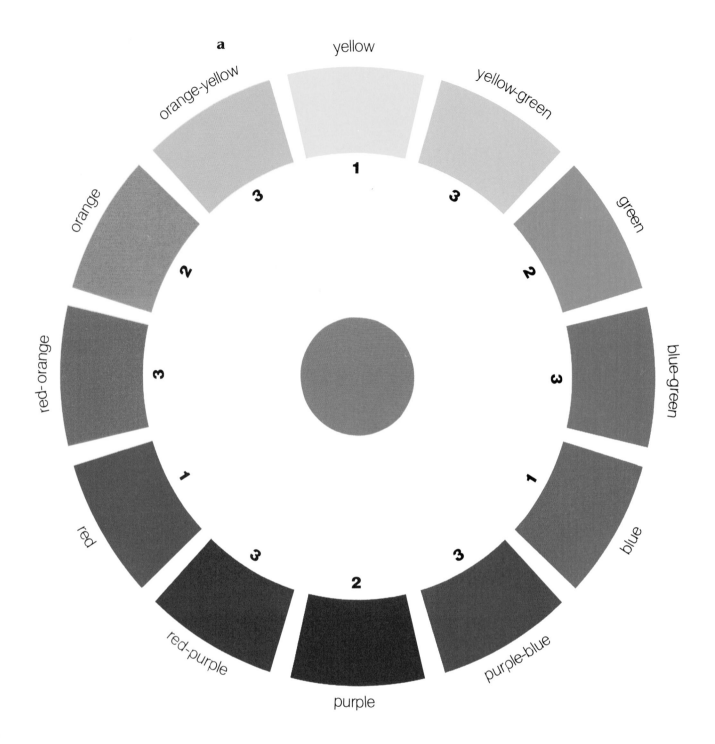

Properties of Color

Color/Value

Hue

The first property of color is what we call *hue.* Hue simply refers to the name of the color. Red, orange, green, and purple are hues. There are relatively few actual color names. Confusion exists because in the world of commercial products, color names abound; Plum, Adobe, Colonial Blue, Desert Sunset, Mayan Gold, and Avocado are a few examples. These often romantic images are extremely inexact terms that mean only what the manufacturers think they mean. The same hue can have dozens of different commercial names.

Example **a** shows what is called a *color wheel,* the most common organization of the basic colors. The wheel system dates back to the early 18th century. This particular organization uses twelve hues, which are divided into three categories:

The three *primary* (1) colors are red, yellow, and blue. From these, all other colors are mixed.

The three *secondary* (2) colors are mixtures of the two primaries: red and yellow make orange, yellow and blue make green, blue and red make purple. Because of the relative strength of the various hues, a visual middle secondary is not always *equal* amounts of the two colors.

The six *tertiary* (3) colors are mixtures of a primary and an adjacent secondary: blue and green make blue-green, red and purple make red-purple, and so on.

It should be noted that this color wheel applies to *pigment,* not light. In a combination of various colors of light, the resulting hues could be entirely different from those illustrated here.

This layout of twelve hues is purely arbitrary, as is this choice of primary colors. Two other color systems are shown just for comparison. Example **b** diagrams the Munsell color organization, (**c**) the Ostwald wheel. Both of these cite different primary colors. The Munsell system involves the five primaries shown, with five "intermediates" (red plus yellow does not produce "orange," but the intermediate "yellow-red") and a complete wheel of one hundred hues. The Ostwald wheel is based on four primaries, with a total of twenty-four hues on the complete wheel. All these color organizations are satisfactory, although one might be preferred for a specific color problem. This book will use the basic twelve-color wheel because it works perfectly well for most design problems involving the usual pigment or dye.

a Color wheel showing primary, secondary, and tertiary colors.
b The Munsell color system.
c The Ostwald color system.

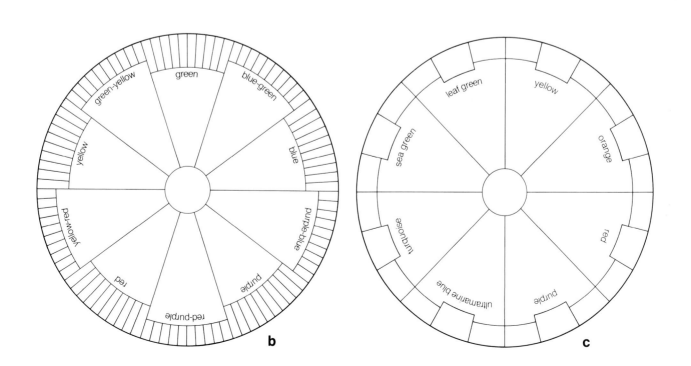

b

c

Color/Value

Value

The second property of color is *value*, which refers to the lightness or darkness of the hue. Example **a** shows a value scale of blue. Only one hue is present, but the blue varies widely in light and dark. In pigment, value can be altered by adding white or black paint to the color. Adding white lightens the color and produces a *tint*, or high-value color. Adding black darkens the color and produces a *shade*, or low-value color. Individual perception varies, but most people can distinguish at least forty tints and shades of any color.

Not all the colors on the color wheel are shown at the same value. Each is shown at *normal* value, with the pure color unmixed and undiluted. The normal values of yellow and of blue, for example, are radically different. Since yellow is a light, or high-value, color, a yellow value

scale would show many more shades than tints. The blue scale (**a**) shows more tints, since normal blue is darker than middle value.

Value, like color itself, is variable and entirely dependent on surrounding hues for its visual sensation. In example **a** a value scale of seven blues from dark to light, the center circle in each area is a constant middle-value blue, but its value appears to change depending on the square in which it is placed. The center circle seems much darker on the lighter blues than on the darker ones. In **b** the center green area appears much darker on the white background than on the black.

Colors being changed by their context is a well-known occurrence. Many authors have termed this the *spreading effect*, where the color sensation "spreads" to affect the adjacent hues. Often artists have outlined their colored areas with black line. It has been observed that this

technique does make the enclosed color seem visually richer and clearer in tone. The dark separating form seems to inhibit the spreading effect and lets each color display its characteristic sensation independently.

In stained glass, the dark black leading around the colored glass segments is a structural necessity to hold the pieces in place. The unusual color brilliance of the Byzantine mosaics (**c**) has been attributed to the slight dark lines that enclose each brightly colored tile. Outlining colored forms in dark lines is common to many periods of art and many media, such as painting, where there is no real functional reason to include them. In eras when a naturalistic, purely visual image was desired, outlining was condemned as unrealistic and "primitive," but it has served as a valuable artistic device to enhance color over the centuries, including 20th-century art.

Incidentally, an outline in white or a light-value color (**d**) achieves the opposite effect. The enclosed color now seems less rich, less dynamic, and jewel-like. The white apparently "spreads" to lend a slightly washed-out or tinted effect to the outlined hue.

a The blue scale shows variations in value from white to black. The circles in the centers are all middle value, although they seem different against lighter or darker backgrounds.
b When colors are seen in conjunction with one another, they appear to change in value.
c *Theodora and Attendants*, detail of Empress Theodora. c. 547. Apse mosaic, San Vitale, Ravenna.
d Guillaume Beverloo Corneille. *Discovery of the Island.* 1965. Oil on canvas, 31⅝ × 25⅜" (80 × 64 cm). Private collection.

b

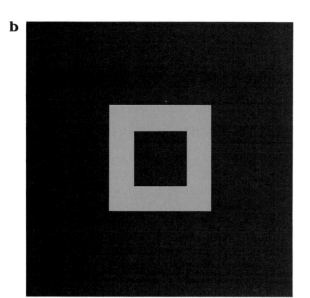 

c

d

Color/Value

Intensity/Complementary Colors

The third property of color is *intensity,* which refers to the brightness of a color. Since a color is at full intensity only when pure and unmixed, a relationship exists between *value* and *intensity.* Mixing black or white with a color changes its value, but at the same time affects its intensity. To see the distinction between the two terms, look at the two tints (high value) of red in example **a**. The tints have about the same degree of lightness, yet one might be called "rose," the other "shocking pink." The two colors are very different in their visual effect, and the difference comes from brightness or intensity. Intensity is sometimes called *chroma,* or *saturation.*

There are two ways to lower the intensity of a color—to make a color less bright, more neutral and dull. One way is to mix gray with the color.

Depending on the gray used, you can dull a color without changing its value. The second way is to mix a color with its *complement,* the color directly across from it on the color wheel. Example **b** shows an intensity scale involving the complementary colors blue and orange. Neutralized (low-intensity) versions of a color are often called *tones.* In **b** we see three tones of blue and three tones of orange. As progressively more orange is added to the blue, the blue becomes duller, more grayed. The same is true of the orange, which becomes more brown as blue is added. When complements are mixed in equal amounts, they cancel each other out, and a muddy neutral tone results.

Complementary colors are direct opposites in position and in character. Mixing complementary colors together dulls them, but when complementary colors are placed *next to each other,* they intensify each oth-

er's brightness. When blue and orange are side by side, each color will appear brighter than in any other context. This effect is called *simultaneous contrast,* meaning that each complement simultaneously intensifies the visual brilliance of the other, so that the colors appear to vibrate. Artists use this visual effect when they wish to produce brilliant color effects. The marvelous Art Nouveau tapestry in **c** effectively employs complementary colors. Here the weirdly flowing red shapes of the angels' dresses contrast with the flat areas of grass in complementary green. The small round purple shapes of the far background trees stand out vividly against the complementary yellow sky.

Another peculiar visual phenomenon of complementary colors is called *afterimage.* Stare at an area of intense color for a minute or so, and then glance away at a white piece of paper or wall. Suddenly, an area of the complementary color will seem to appear. For example, when you look at the white wall after staring at a red shape, a definite green area in the same shape will seem to take form on the wall.

a Two tints of red at the same value have different intensities.
b One way to lower the intensity of a color is to mix it with its complement.
c Henry van de Velde. *Engelwache (Angel Vigil).* 1893. Tapestry, 4'6⅜" × 7'6⅞" (1.4 × 2.33 m). Museum Bellerive, Zurich.

a

b

c

a

b

Optical Color Mixing

Color/Value

The color green can be made by mixing blue and yellow pigment. The artist on his palette mixes many different greens, depending on the amount of each primary used. Instead of *mixing* the colors, a green area may be created by placing random small dots of the *pure* yellow and blue side by side. A similar effect can be created by painting an area of yellow, then lightly dragging a coat of blue on top, allowing flecks of the yellow underneath to be seen. In these cases, the viewer's eye from a certain distance does the "mixing," and a green image results. This is called *optical mixing,* or sometimes *retinal fusion.* Whether this green will seem more intense and brilliant than the pre-mixed pigment is often debated. Mixing various colors of paint to produce other colors (called the *additive* process) can often result in neutral, even "muddy" colors. Some artists have felt that the process of optical mixing avoided this result and produced visually brighter colors. Other artists (such as Matisse) have believed that the color effect was weakened and rejected the technique in their paintings.

The technique of optical mixing is often used in creating mosaics. Stirring up a bowl of yellow and blue tiles will not, of course, produce green tesserae. Instead, small pieces of pure-colored tiles are interspersed to produce the effect of many other intermediate colors. The same process is employed in creating tapestries. Weavers working with a limited number of colored yarns or threads can intermingle them, so that at a distance the eye merges them and creates an impression of many hues and values (**a**).

The process of optical mixing applies as well to the field of painting, notably in the work of the 19th-century Impressionists. If we view a painting such as that by Monet (**b**) from a very close range, it seems almost a disjointed pattern of small splotches of paint. But when we back off, these dabs of paint unite to form areas of intense color. With their interest in reproducing the visual effects of light and atmosphere, the Impressionists found optical mixing a valuable technique.

The Post-Impressionist Georges Seurat used a style called *pointillism* ("points," or small dots of color) which employed the same optical mixing of color. This pointillist technique is now used everyday in a photomechanical adaptation in the printing of color pictures. The numerous colors we see in printed reproductions are all produced by usually just four basic colors in a small dot pattern. The dots in this case are so tiny that we are totally unaware of them unless we use a magnifying glass to visually enlarge them (**c**).

a Workshop of Nicolas Bataille. *King Arthur,* detail from the *Nine Heroes* series. c. 1385. Tapestry, entire work 9'11¾" × 11'6¼" (3.04 × 3.51 m). Metropolitan Museum of Art, New York (Cloisters Collection, Munsey Fund, 1932).

b Claude Monet. *Poplars on the Bank of the Epte River.* 1891. Oil on canvas, 39½ × 25¾" (100 × 65 cm). Philadelphia Museum of Art (bequest of Anne Thomson as a memorial to her father, Frank Thomson, and her mother, Mary Elizabeth Clarke Thomson).

c Photograph with enlarged photomechanical dot pattern showing blending into different colors.

c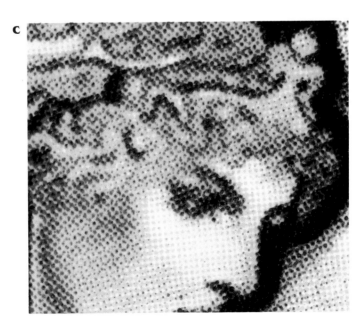

Cool/Warm Colors

Color/Value

Cool colors? *Warm* colors? These may seem odd adjectives to apply to the visual sensation of color, as "cool" and "warm" are sensations of touch, not sight. Nevertheless, we are all familiar with the terms and continually refer to colors this way. Because of the learned association of color and objects, we continue to identify and relate the sensations of the different senses. Hence, red and orange (fire) and yellow (sunlight) become identified as warm colors. Similarly, blue (sky, water) and green (grass, forest) are always thought of as cool colors.

Touching an area of red will assuredly not burn your hand, but *looking* at red will indeed induce a feeling of warmth. The effect may be purely psychological, but the results are very real. We have all read of the workers in an office painted blue complaining of the chill and actually getting colds. The problem was solved not by raising the thermostat, but by repainting the office in warm tones of brown. The turn-of-the-century illustrator Maxfield Parrish makes us feel the cool, restful tranquillity of the forest by limiting his color choices to the blue side of the spectrum (**a**).

On the color wheel, the tertiary red-orange appears as the warmest color, and the opposite blue-green seems the coldest of the hues. We generally think of yellow through red-violet as the warm side of the color wheel and yellow-green through violet as the cool segment. The visual effects are quite variable, however, and again depend a great deal on the context in which we see the color. In **b** the green square appears very warm surrounded by a background of blue. But in **c** the identical green, when placed on an orange background, shifts and becomes a cooler tone.

As warm colors tend to advance, while cool colors seem to recede, the artist may use the warm/cool relationship to establish a feeling of depth and volume. Probably no group of artists has investigated and expanded our ideas of color more than the Impressionists. The blue and purple shadows (instead of gray and black) that so shocked the 19th-century public seem to us today perfectly logical and reasonable. In Renoir's still life (**d**), *Fruits of the Midi,* notice how the rounded volumes are molded by the artist's use of warm and cool contrasts. The highlights in warm tones gradually change to cooler colors expressing the shadow areas.

a Maxfield Parrish. *Scribner's Fiction Number.* 1897. Poster. Victoria and Albert Museum, London.
b A colored area on a cool background will appear warmer in tone.
c The same color surrounded by a warm background seems cool.
d Auguste Renoir. *Fruits of the Midi.* 1881. Oil on canvas, 20 × 27″ (51 × 69 cm). Art Institute of Chicago (Mr. and Mrs. Martin A. Ryerson).

d

a

b

c

Color and Space

There is a direct relationship between color and a visual impression of depth, or pictorial space. Colors have an innate advancing or receding quality because of slight muscular reactions in our eyes as we focus on different colors. Intense, warm colors (red, orange, yellow) seem to come forward; cool colors (blue, green) seem to go back. In addition, the dust in the earth's atmosphere breaks up the color rays from distant objects and makes them appear bluish. As objects recede, any brilliance of color becomes more neutral, finally seeming to be gray-blue.

Artists can use color's spatial properties to create either an illusion of depth or a flat, one-dimensional pattern. The Durand landscape in **a** gives a feeling of great distance. The overlapping planes of the hills become grayer and more bluish in color as they extend farther back from the figures in the foreground. In contrast, Bonnard's painting **(b)** shows the central background hill as a brilliant, advancing orange that denies the implicit depth and creates a flatter decorative effect.

Even in a still-life painting the spatial quality can be emphasized or ignored. In **c** de Heem has played up a feeling of depth. While the bright reds and yellows of the fruit tend to advance, the neutral browns and grays of the wall recede. To heighten this effect, the artist gives us a glimpse of landscape through a window, extending far back in grayish blues. On the other hand, Matisse in his still life **(d)** consciously flattens and compresses space by the use of brilliant, warm colors and strong dark- and light-value patterns in background areas that would ordinarily recede. An exuberant but very flat painting results.

Color values are also important in spatial illusion. Whatever the colors used, high contrast comes forward visually, while areas of lesser contrast generally recede.

a Asher Durand. *Kindred Spirits.* 1849. Oil on canvas, 46 × 36″ (117 × 92 cm). New York Public Library (Astor, Lenox, and Tilden Foundations).
b Pierre Bonnard. *Mediterranean Coast.* c. 1943. Oil on canvas, 37¾ × 28½″ (96 × 72 cm). Collection Phillips Family.
c Jan Davidsz de Heem. *Still Life with a View of Antwerp.* 1646. Oil on canvas, 23⅜ × 36½″ (59 × 93 cm). Toledo Museum of Art (gift of Edward Drummond Libbey).
d Henri Matisse. *Still Life in the Studio, Interior at Nice.* 1924. Oil on canvas, 39½ × 31½″ (100.5 × 80 cm). Private collection.

d

Color/Value

Color Schemes

Monochromatic, Analogous, Complementary, Triadic

There are four basic color schemes (or color harmonies, as they are often called).

A *monochromatic* color scheme involves the use of only one hue **(a)**. The hue can vary in value, and pure black or white may be added. The visual effect is extremely harmonious and generally quiet, restful, and (depending on the range of values) subtle.

An *analogous* color scheme combines several hues that sit next to each other on the color wheel. Again, the hues may vary in value. Example **b**, a painting by Cézanne, shows the related harmonious feeling that analogous color lends to a painting.

A *complementary* color scheme, as the term implies, joins colors opposite each other on the color wheel. This combination will produce a lively, exciting pattern, especially with the colors at full intensity. The blue and orange in Davis' painting **(c)** bring a vibrant contrast of color, more dynamic than that in **b**.

A *triadic* color scheme involves three hues equally spaced on the color wheel. Red, yellow, and blue would be the most common example **(d)**. Since the hues come from different parts of the wheel, the result is again contrasting and lively.

These color schemes are probably more applicable to such design areas as interiors, posters, and packaging than to painting.

In painting, color often is used intuitively, and many artists would reject the idea that they work by formula. But knowing these harmonies can help designers to consciously plan the visual effects they wish a finished pattern to have. Moreover, color can easily provide a visual unity that might not be obvious in the initial pattern of shapes. While design aims vary, often the more complicated and "busy" the pattern of shapes, the more useful will be a strict control of the color—and the reverse.

Color unity is described by another term. We often speak of the *tonality* of a design or painting. *Tonality* refers to the dominance of a single color or the visual importance of a hue that seems to pervade the whole color structure despite the presence of other colors. Monochromatic patterns (as value studies in one color) give a uniform tonality, since only one hue is present. Analogous color schemes can also produce a dominant tonality, as **b** shows. When colors are chosen from one part of the color wheel, they will share one hue in common. Yellow-green, blue-green, blue, and blue-purple all derive from the primary blue, so they yield a blue tonality in **b**.

a Josef Albers. *Homage to the Square, White Line Square XIII.* 1967. Lithograph, 20¾" (53 cm) square. Collection Mrs. Anni Albers and the Josef Albers Foundation, Inc.

b Paul Cézanne. *Le Lac d'Annecy.* 1896. Oil on canvas, 25 × 31½" (64 × 80 cm). Courtauld Institute Galleries, London (Courtauld Collection).

c Stuart Davis. *Colonial Cubism.* 1954. Oil on canvas, 3'9" × 5'1⅛" (1.14 × 1.53 m). Walker Art Center, Minneapolis (gift of T. B. Walker Foundation).

d Charles Demuth. *Buildings Abstraction, Lancaster.* 1931. Oil on board, 27⅞ × 23⅝" (71 × 60 cm). Detroit Institute of Art (Founders Society Purchase, General Membership Fund).

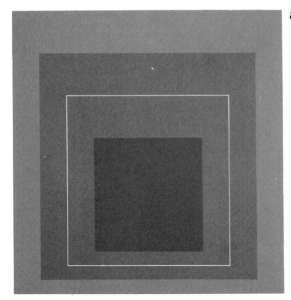

a

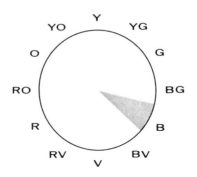

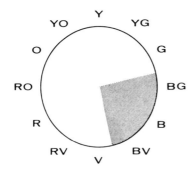

b

c

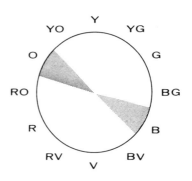

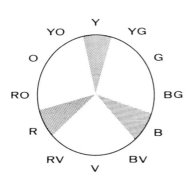

d

Color/Value

Color Discord

Color *discord* is the opposite of color harmony. A combination of discordant colors is visually disturbing, for the colors have no basic affinity for each other. They seem to clash, to pull away in opposing directions, rather than to relate harmoniously to one another. The term "discord" conveys an immediate negative impression. Discord in life, in a personal relationship, may certainly not be pleasant, but it often provides excitement. In the same manner, discord can be extremely useful in art and design.

Mild discord results in exciting, eye-catching color combinations. The world of fashion has exploited the idea to the point that mildly discordant combinations are almost commonplace. A discordant color note in a painting or design may contribute visual surprise and also better express certain themes or ideas. A poster may attract attention by its startling colors.

Once rules were taught about just which color combinations were harmonious and which were definitely to be avoided because the colors did not "go together." A combination of pink and orange was unthinkable; even blue and green patterns were suspect. Today, these rules seem silly, and we approach color more freely, seeking unexpected combinations.

Colors widely separated on the color wheel (but *not* complements) are generally seen as discordant combinations. The following combinations will produce visual discord and are illustrated here.

Example **a** combines a primary and a tertiary beyond an adjacent secondary: red and blue-purple.

Example **b** combines a secondary and a tertiary beyond an adjacent primary: orange and yellow-green.

Example **c** combines two tertiaries on either side of a primary: blue-green and blue-purple.

In producing discord, value is an important consideration. As **d** shows, the impression of discord is much greater when the value of the two colors is similar. With great dark and light contrast between the hues, few color combinations will look truly unpleasant. But when the value contrast is absent, we begin to see the actual disharmony of the hues.

The painting by Franz Marc (**e**) has many areas where purposely discordant colors are placed together. Hence, the effect is visually unsettling.

a Red and blue-purple.
b Orange and yellow-green.
c Blue-green and blue-purple.
d Pure orange and two shades of red-purple.
e Franz Marc. *The Yellow Cow.* 1911. Oil on canvas, 4'7⅜" × 6'2½" (1.41 × 1.89 m). Solomon R. Guggenheim Museum, New York.

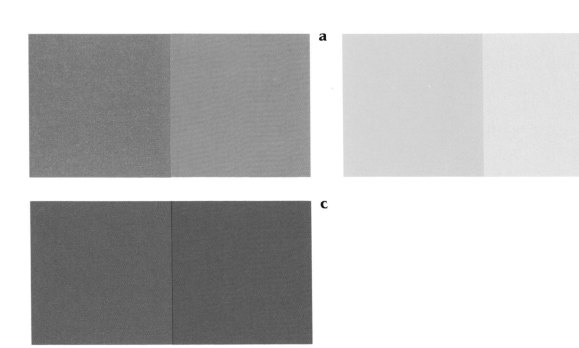

a

b

c

d

e

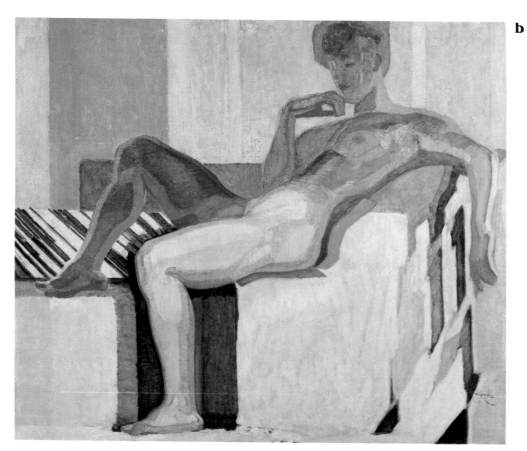

Color Uses

Color/Value

Local, Optical, Arbitrary

There are three basic ways in which color can be used in painting.

An artist may use what is called *local* color. This term refers to the identifying color of an object under ordinary daylight. Local color is the objective color that we "know" objects are: grass is green, bananas are yellow, apples are red. The artist controls the color scheme mainly by the mental identification of the colors in the subject matter.

Visually, the red of an apple can change radically, depending on the illumination. Since color is a property of light, the color of any object changes at sunset, under moonlight, or by candlelight as in **a**. Even atmospheric effects can visually change the local color of distant objects such as faraway mountains appearing blue. An artist reproducing these visual effects is using *optical* color.

In *arbitrary* color, the color choices are subjective, rather than based on the colors seen in nature. The artists' colors are selected for design, aesthetic, or emotional reasons. The colors in Kupka's painting **(b)** were chosen for their spatial and decorative qualities, not for any objective reference to the natural colors of a nude woman. Arbitrary color is sometimes difficult to pinpoint because many painters take some artistic liberties in using color. Has the artist disregarded the colors he saw or has he merely intensified and exaggerated the visual reference? This latter use is termed *heightened* color. Albert Marquet's painting of Paris **(c)** is an example. Late on an overcast afternoon, the shadows in the city could well have a slightly blue or purple cast. Marquet has exagger-

ated, or "heightened," this visual effect.

Pure arbitrary (or subjective) color is often seen in 20th-century painting. Just as art in general has moved away from naturalism, so has arbitrary color tended to become an important interest. Even color photography—with filters, infrared film, and various darkroom techniques—has experimented widely in the area of unexpected color effects.

These categories of color use obviously apply to paintings with identifiable subject matter. In nonobjective art the forms have no apparent reference to natural objects, so that the color is also nonobjective. Purely aesthetic considerations determine the color choices.

---

a Georges de la Tour. *The Repentant Magdalen.* c. 1640. Oil on canvas, 14½ × 36½" (37 × 93 cm). National Gallery of Art, Washington, DC (Ailsa Mellon Bruce Fund, 1974).

b Frantisek Kupka. *Planes by Color, Large Nude.* 1909. Oil on canvas, 4'10⅝" × 5'10⅛" (1.49 × 1.78 m). Solomon R. Guggenheim Museum, New York.

c Albert Marquet. *The Pont Neuf.* 1906. Oil on canvas, 19¾ × 24⅛" (50 × 61 cm). National Gallery of Art, Washington, DC (Chester Dale Collection, 1962).

c

Color/Value

Emotional Color

"Ever since our argument, I've been blue."

"I saw red *when she lied to me."*

"You're certainly in a black *mood today."*

"I was green *with envy when I saw their new house."*

These statements are emotional. The speakers are expressing an emotional reaction, and somehow a color reference makes the meaning clearer, since color appeals to our emotions and feelings. For artists who wish to arouse an emotional response in the viewer, color is the most effective element. Even before we "read" the subject matter or iden-

tify the forms, the color creates an atmosphere to which we respond.

In a very basic instance, we commonly recognize so-called warm and cool colors. Yellows, oranges, and reds give us an instinctive feeling of warmth and evoke warm, happy, cheerful reactions. Cooler blues and greens are automatically associated with quieter, less outgoing feelings and can express melancholy **(a)** or depression. These are generalities, of course, for the combination of colors is vital, and the artist can also influence our reactions by the values and intensities of the colors selected.

Paintings in which color causes an emotional reaction and relates to the thematic subject matter are very common. But notice the difference that color *alone* can make in our

emotional reaction to a painting. Examples **b** and **c** are nonobjective; there is *no* subject matter. Yet what a different feeling each work gives us because of the color choices. The reddish areas overlaid with foreboding heavy strokes of black in Soulages' *Peinture, 13 février 1960* **(c)** give an immediate dark, ominous emotional feeling without any subject reference. By contrast, the complementary blue and orange in Hofmann's painting **(b)** are vibrantly alive. These clean, sparkling, bright colors give an instantly cheerful, pleasant effect.

It is interesting to note how the feeling of shape can be related to color. A jagged, angular, dynamic shape in a soft grayish-lavender can seem like a design contradiction. It is generally more satisfactory to select colors that relate to the emotional qualities already present in the shapes (or vice versa). All elements of a design should work together unless a deliberate incongruity (or visual confusion) is the desired effect.

a Pablo Picasso. *Two Women Seated at a Bar.* 1902. Oil on canvas, 31½ × 36¼" (80 × 92 cm). Private collection.

b Hans Hofmann. *The Golden Wall.* 1961. Oil on canvas, 5' × 6'½" (1.5 × 1.84 m). Art Institute of Chicago (Mr. and Mrs. Frank G. Logan Prize Fund).

c Pierre Soulages. *Peinture, 13 Février 1960.* 1960. Oil on canvas, 3'8½" × 4'9" (1.13 × 1.45 m). Collection Sigrid Freundorfer, New York.

a

Color/Value

Color Symbolism

"Don't worry, he's true blue."

"I caught him red-handed."

"So I told her a little white lie."

"Why not just admit you're too yellow to do it?"

We frequently utter statements that employ color references to describe character traits or human behavior. These color references are *symbolic.* The colors in the above statements symbolize abstract concepts or ideas: fidelity, sin, innocence, and cowardice. The colors do not stand for tangibles like fire, grass, water, or even sunlight. They represent mental, conceptual qualities. The colors chosen to symbolize various ideas are often arbitrary, or the initial reasons for their choice are so buried in history we no longer remember them. Can we really explain why green means "go" and red signifies "stop"?

A main point to remember is that symbolic color references are cultural: they are not worldwide, but vary from one society to another. What is the color of mourning that one associates with a funeral? In our society one would say black, but the answer would be white in India, violet in Turkey, brown in Ethiopia, and yellow in Burma. What is the color of royalty? We think of purple (dating back to the Egyptians), but the royal color was yellow in dynastic China and red in ancient Rome (a custom continued today in the cardinals' robes of the Catholic Church). What does a bride wear? White is our response, but yellow is the choice in Hindu India and red in China.

Different eras and different cultures invent different color symbols.

The symbolic use of color was very important in ancient art for identifying specific figures or deities to an illiterate public. Not only the ancients used color in this manner. In the countless pictures of the Virgin Mary through centuries of Western art, she is very rarely not shown in a blue robe over a red or white dress.

Symbolic color designations are less important in art than they once were. Still, they linger on and can help an artist to create designs on specific themes. The dominant red-orange with discordant bits of red-purple in the poster in **a** symbolizes the opera's gruesome theme of insanity and murder as well as the composer's atonal music, with its lack of traditional musical harmony.

a Jan Lenica. *Alban Berg Wozzeck.* 1964. Offset lithograph, 38⅛ × 26½" (97 × 67 cm). Museum of Modern Art, New York (anonymous gift).

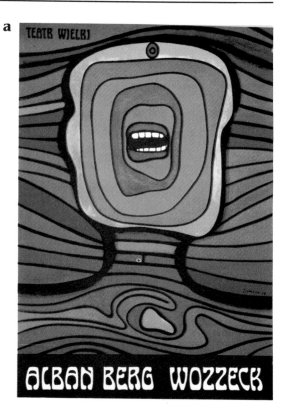

Color vs. Value

We customarily think of an artist as working with color. But consider the vast area of drawings, woodcuts, etchings, and lithographs produced using pure value and no color. Also consider fields such as sculpture and architecture. Here, while color is present, the main design consideration has often been value because of the usual monotone of the materials involved. And texture, which is so important an element in these fields, is essentially a variation in light and dark visual patterns. It would seem that an artist in almost any field or specialization should be skillful in manipulating both color and value.

Do color and value work together or at cross-purposes? This may seem like a nonsensical question, but it has been argued over the centuries. Some critics have maintained that the emphasis in a work should be on one *or* the other. Some artists of the past seemingly felt this way also. Leonardo da Vinci called color the "greatest enemy of art," and Titian supposedly said that an artist needs only three colors. Obviously, these artists were content to rely on value changes, rather than contrast of pure color. The Fauves and Expressionists of the 20th century would undoubtedly agree with van Gogh's statement that "Coloring is what makes a painter a painter."

Historically, it seems that, for whatever reason, many artists have often chosen to put the emphasis on either color or value. And art historians outlining the stylistic changes in art have described shifts in this area as indicative of a new period.

If we cannot see a work of art first-hand, nothing gives us as faithful an impression of the original as a photograph in full color. In any work, the color (even the paper color in a drawing) adds to our pleasure and understanding. But black-and-white reproductions are a practical and economic necessity. This changing of color/value emphasis among different artists and different periods would explain why some works seem so inadequate when shown in a black-and-white illustration. A book on Impressionism, for example, without any illustrations in color would be impossible; it could barely hint at the sparkle, richness, and brilliance of the original paintings. But a Renaissance painting is satisfactory, if not satisfying, shown only in value. In 20th-century art, Color Field painting loses its whole impetus when devoid of color; Super-Realism can be appreciated without color, just as a black-and-white photograph *can* substitute for one in color.

It is doubtful that any instructor or critic today would ask artists to make a flat-out, definitive choice between color and value as the point of emphasis in their work. But it is intriguing that such a choice (conscious or intuitive) was apparently made by many great artists.

11

Illusion
of Motion

a

b

Introduction

Illusion of Motion

Examples **a** and **b** are completely different forms of visual art. They were produced by very different artists in very different societies in different centuries for very different purposes. Yet they share one common basic aim. Both are attempts to portray a feeling of *movement* by showing a series of images that imply motion and passage of time between episodes.

In a comic strip such as "Peanuts" **(a)**, we follow a character through a series of situations that relate a story. Example **b** has the same idea, though the format is not broken into separate panels. In Sassetta's painting, we see the main character, St. Anthony, in three situations. At upper left he embarks on his travels; at upper right he encounters a centaur, which he blesses; in the closest area, at lower right, he ultimately arrives at his meeting with St. Paul, whom he embraces. Very dissimilar images have the same goal—an illusion of motion.

In any of the three-dimensional arts, such as sculpture and architecture, much of the observer's visual pleasure has come from moving about and looking at the work from different angles. But some art forms themselves move, and we apply the term *kinetic* to them. Kinetic sculpture moves, although we may stand still. While not unknown in history, the idea of kinetic sculpture has become increasingly important in the past few decades. We are all familiar with mobiles, hanging constructions of shapes and wires that are designed to turn and revolve, presenting a constantly changing visual pattern. The relationship of the shapes is always shifting and creating new designs. Today many sculptures have motors, blinking lights, and other moving parts to present this art-in-motion concept. The sculpture in **c** combines the idea of a machine with the pleasures of a fountain of flowing water. Various abstract volumes fill with water, then overturn (spilling the water), and begin to fill again. A constantly changing and moving design is intriguing to watch.

a "Peanuts" by Charles M. Schulz. © 1968 by United Feature Syndicate.
b Sassetta. *Meeting of St. Anthony and St. Paul the Hermit.* 1430–32. Panel, 18¾ × 13⅝"
(48 × 35 cm). National Gallery of Art, Washington, DC (Samuel H. Kress Collection).
c Lin Emery. *Homage to Amercreo.* 1964. Wood. 6′8″ high (2.03 m).
American Creosote Works, Inc., New Orleans.

c

a

b

c

Introduction

Illusion of Motion

There have been many attempts to inject some feeling of motion into the essentially static images of two-dimensional drawings and paintings. In this case, the movement is merely an illusion, a suggestion when actual motion is not possible. Why do artists attempt this illusion of motion, a quality that patently cannot be present? The reason is that change and movement are essential characteristics of our world. We humans cannot sit or stand motionless for more than a moment or so; even in sleep we turn and change position. But if we could stop our body movements, the world about us would still continue to change.

Ever since prehistoric times this dynamic quality of our world has been noticed. When the Paleolithic cave dwellers first drew pictures on their cave walls, their images of animals were often portrayed with the front and rear legs extended in positions of movement (**a**). These primitive artists recognized an essential characteristic of animals: they run

and move. Many subsequent artists also have attempted to reflect the idea of motion (**b**).

Presenting an illusion of motion is, like most aspects of art, an option for the artist. Some artists strive for it; others purposely ignore it. In the periods of art commonly styled *classical*, the whole concept of motion was consciously rejected. Classical art aimed to create unemotional, reserved images that would have an ageless permanent quality. A suggestion of anything momentary or temporary was rejected. These idealized forms exuded an air of unchanging stability, devoid of motion. The

Raphael painting in **c** is an example of this approach. Raphael's exquisitely graceful, relaxed figures are posed in an idyllic landscape. No hint of change disturbs their serenity.

The *Super-Realist* painting in **d** is clearly very different. The construction workers are in poses that we immediately recognize as momentary and bound to change in another second. The worker at the right is taking off his shirt and obviously will not be in this position for more than a moment. Despite the meticulous technique of the rendering, we immediately infer a feeling of change and motion from painting **d**.

---

a *Hall of Bulls*, left wall, Lascaux. c. 15,000–10,000 B.C. Dordogne, France.
b Giacomo Balla. *Dynamism of a Dog on a Leash*. 1912. Oil on canvas, 35⅜ × 43¼″ (90 × 110 cm). Albright-Knox Art Gallery, Buffalo, NY (Bequest of A. Conger Goodyear to George F. Goodyear, life interest, and Albright-Knox Art Gallery, 1964).
c Raphael. *The Alba Madonna*. c. 1510. Oil transferred from wood to canvas, diameter 37¼″ (95 cm). National Gallery of Art, Washington, DC (Andrew W. Mellon Collection).
d Michael Leonard. *The Scaffolders*. 1978. Acrylic on canvas, 41 × 40″ (104 × 102 cm). Courtesy Fischer Fine Art Ltd., London.

d

Illusion of Motion

Anticipated Movement

Much of the implication of movement present in art is caused by our memory and past experience. We recognize temporary, unstable body positions and realize that change must be imminent. We immediately "see" the action portrayed in a section from the Bayeux Tapestry (**a**). From the positions of the bodies and the horses, we anticipate the violent movement taking place. Also, in a process called *kinesthetic empathy*, we tend to recreate unconsciously in our own bodies the actions we observe. We actually *feel* in our muscles the exertions of the athlete or dancer;

we simultaneously stretch, push, or lean, though we are only watching. This involuntary reaction also applies to static images in art, where it can enhance the feeling of movement.

A feeling of movement can be heightened by contrast. Again, by memory, we realize that some things move and some do not. Thus, in **b** the figures seem to have more activity, more potential of movement, in their active positions because of the contrast with the large stolid building that appears so immobile. Our experience tells us that people move, but buildings rarely do.

Even nonobjective patterns can display movement through contrast. Because of past experience, we also see horizontal lines as quiet and inactive—just as our bodies are resting and still when we are lying horizontally. For a similar reason, we identify diagonal lines as suggestive of movement—just as our bodies lean and bend in such vigorous activities as sports. The horizontal emphasis of the building in **b** imparts a static feeling. But pure lines without subject reference can give the same result. Thus, Mondrian's paintings, with their constant repetition of stabilizing horizontal and vertical lines, seem static and unmoving. In contrast, a painting such as **c** is a dynamic, motion-filled image solely because of the emphasis on diagonal movement and vigorous brushstrokes.

a *Climax of the Battle of Hastings,* detail of the *Bayeux Tapestry.* c. 1073–88. Wool embroidery on linen; height 1′8″ (0.51 m), overall length 231′ (70.41 m). Town Hall, Bayeux.
b Nicolas Poussin. *The Rape of the Sabine Women.* c. 1636–37. Oil on canvas, 5′1″ × 6′10½″ (1.55 × 2.1 m). Metropolitan Museum of Art, New York (Harris Brisbane Dick Fund).
c Michael Larionov. *Rayonist Composition: Domination of Red.* 1912–13. Oil on canvas, 20¾ × 28½″ (53 × 72 cm). Museum of Modern Art, New York (gift of the artist).

a

b

c

Illusion of Motion

Over the centuries, artists have devised various conventions to present an illusion of motion in art. One of the oldest devices is that of *repeating a figure*. As the Indian miniature in **a** illustrates, the figure of Krishna appears over and over in different positions and situations. This device was used widely in Western medieval art (**b**), as well as in most Oriental cultures. It is interesting to note that this very old technique is still popular. Any time a figure is repeated, as in the double-image portrait in **c**, a feeling of movement results.

Often the repeated figure, rather than being shown in a sequence of small pictures, merely reappears in one unified composition. This device occurred in Oriental art, was adopted in Western art, and remained popular as late as the Renaissance. Usually, a distinctive costume or color identified the repeated character, so that the repetition would be visually obvious. The effect can be quite subtle, as in *The Tribute Money* (**d**), painted about 1427. The tax collector demands the tribute money of Christ in the center, as Christ tells Peter to get the money from the fish's mouth. On the left Peter kneels to get the money, and on the right he pays it to the tax collector. Without more than casual observation, however, we might miss the important sequential aspect.

a *Krishna Revealing His Nature as Vishnu.* Miniature from Malwa, India. c. 1730. Gouache or watercolor on paper, 8 × 14¾″ (20 × 38 cm). Victoria & Albert Museum, London (Crown Copyright).

b Scenes from the life of St. Paul, from the *Bible of Charles the Bald.* c. 875–77. Manuscript illumination. St. Paul Outside the Walls, Rome.

c Larry Rivers. *Double Portrait of Birdie.* 1955. Oil on canvas, 5′10¾″ × 6′10½″ (1.8 × 2.1 m). Whitney Museum of American Art, New York (anonymous gift).

d Masaccio. *The Tribute Money.* c. 1427. Fresco, 8′4″ × 19′8″ (2.54 × 5.99 m). Santa Maria del Carmine, Florence.

a

a

b

c

Fuzzy Outlines

Illusion of Motion

We readily interpret a photograph such as the one in **a** as a symbol of movement. With a fast shutter speed, moving images are frozen into "stop-action" photographs. Here the shutter speed is relatively slow, so that the sprinting commuter becomes a blurred, indistinct image that we read as an indication of the subject's movement. This is an everyday visual experience. When objects move through our field of vision quickly, we do not get a clear mental picture of them. A car will pass us on the highway so fast that we perceive only a colored blur. Details and edges of the form are lost in the rapidity of movement.

The two figures in the drawing by the artist Daumier (**b**) suggest movement in this way. They are drawn with sketchy, incomplete, and overlapping lines to define their forms. The figure behind the rail literally wags his finger at the startled lawyer. The hand appears in rapid movement, for we get no one clear view in the blur of motion.

The painting by Renoir in **c** offers an excellent suggestion of motion in the dancing figures and the flicker of gas lamps in a 19th-century dance hall. This movement results mainly from the lack of clear contour lines around the forms. The figures are slightly fuzzy, and many of the forms begin to merge without clear dividing edges.

Even in purely nonobjective paintings, the blurred edge serves as an effective device. The vertical, sweeping shapes in **d** clearly suggest flowing and rapid movement.

a Elliott Erwitt. *Commuter.* 1964. Photograph.
b Honoré Daumier. *The Criminal Case.* n.d. Pen and ink and black chalk, 7⅛ × 11¼″ (18 × 29 cm). Victoria & Albert Museum, London (Crown Copyright).
c Auguste Renoir. *Le Moulin de la Galette.* 1876. Oil on canvas, 4′3½″ × 5′9″ (1.31 × 1.75 m). Louvre, Paris.
d Morris Louis. *Saraband.* 1959. Acrylic on canvas, 8′6″ × 12′5″ (2.57 × 3.78 m). Solomon R. Guggenheim Museum, New York.

d

Illusion of Motion

Multiple Image

Another device for suggesting movement is called *multiple image,* illustrated in **a**. When we see one figure in an overlapping sequence of poses, the slight change in each successive position suggests movement taking place. Example **a** is an old photograph from the 1880s. The photographer, Thomas Eakins, was intrigued with the camera's capabilities for answering the visual problem of showing movement and analyzing it.

Example **b** shows this idea in a drawing by Ingres. While Ingres' motive was probably just to try two different positions for the figure, we get a clear suggestion of the figure moving in dance-like gestures.

Painters of the 20th century have often been concerned with finding a visual language to express the increasingly dynamic quality of the world around us. While at first glance very different, Duchamp's famous

Nude Descending a Staircase (**c**) is actually much like the Eakins photograph (**a**). Again the multiple image of a figure is shown to suggest a body's movement in progress. Now the body forms are highly abstracted into simple geometric forms that repeat diagonally down the canvas as the nude "descends." Many curved lines (called *lines of force*) are added to show the pathway of movement. This is a device we commonly see, and immediately understand, in today's comic strips.

The familiar Venus figure from Botticelli's painting (**d**) has been presented in a new way by Jiří Kolář (**e**). Using the multiple image in a unique manner, **e** repeats parts of the figure over and over in a vertical sequence. The visual effect is a feeling of movement as Venus visually "rises" from the sea.

a Thomas Eakins. *Pole-Vaulter: Multiple-Exposure Photograph of George Reynolds.* c. 1884. Metropolitan Museum of Art, New York (gift of Charles Bregler, 1941).

b Jean Auguste Dominique Ingres. *Female Nude.* c. 1826–34. Pencil on white paper, 10⅞″ × 11½″ (28 × 30 cm). Musée Bonnat, Bayonne.

c Marcel Duchamp. *Nude Descending a Staircase, No. 2.* 1912. Oil on canvas, 4′10″ × 2′11″ (1.47 × 0.89 m). Philadelphia Museum of Art (Louise and Walter Arensberg Collection).

d Sandro Botticelli. *The Birth of Venus,* detail. c. 1480. Oil on canvas, entire work 5′8⅞″ × 9′7⅞″ (1.75 × 2.79 m). Uffizi, Florence.

e Jiří Kolář. *Venus.* 1968. Rollage, 3′5⅜″ × 5′5″ (1.05 × 1.65 m). Courtesy the artist.

a

b

c

NU DESCENDANT L'ESCALIER

d

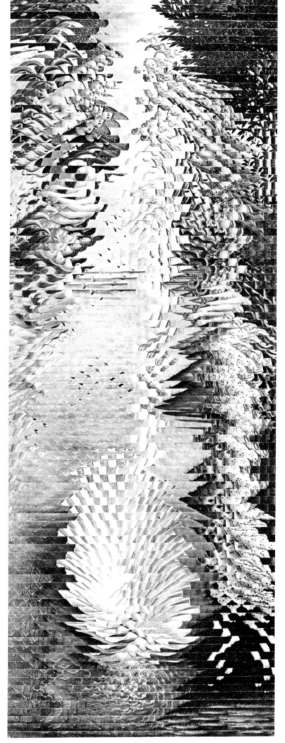
e

a

b

Optical Movement

Illusion of Motion

The paintings illustrated on these pages could scarcely be more different in almost every aspect of art. But, again, they have one element in common: all attempt to give an illusion of motion by *optical movement*. The visual pattern presented literally forces our eyes to keep moving about the painting. This constant eye movement encourages us to feel the dynamic quality inherent in each image.

Rubens, in painting **a**, gives us a very complicated, twisting, and curving linear structure. The contour lines are fairly clear, but they make an extremely busy pattern. Figures bend and gesture wildly, the horse rears up and paws the air, Cupid flies in, a bright red cape flutters out, clouds gather—nowhere is the eye allowed to pause.

In the Rubens painting **(a)** the momentary positions of all the figures reinforce the feeling of motion. In **b** there are no recognizable objects, no forms that we can identify as being fleeting positions. Yet the same optical movement factor is present and perhaps more obvious because of the painting's nonobjective nature. Example **b**, a work by de Kooning, is an example of Abstract Expressionism (so aptly subtitled Action Painting), which makes movement and dynamic excitement as primary goals. The viewer's eye is directed rapidly around the canvas. Moreover, we instantly sense the physical activity of the artist in creating the painting. In **c** the twisting and writhing medieval forms force the eye to wander around the contours, observing the continuous movement of intertwining human and mythological figures.

---

a Peter Paul Rubens. *The Rape of the Daughters of Leucippus.* c. 1618. Oil on canvas, 7′3″ × 6′10″ (2.22 × 2.09 m). Alte Pinakothek, Munich.

b Willem de Kooning. *Composition.* 1955. Oil, enamel, and charcoal on canvas, 6′7⅛″ × 5′9⅛″ (2.01 × 1.76 m). Solomon R. Guggenheim Museum, New York.

c Initial *A* from Manuscript of Josephus. MS Dd.1.4. fol.220r. Canterbury, early 12th century. Reproduced by permission of the Syndics of Cambridge University Library.

c

Illusion of Motion

Op Art

One recent style in art has again concentrated on the idea of movement, but in totally nonobjective terms. This style is popularly called *Op Art*, since the images appeal mainly to the viewer's eye and involve the retina, not the brain or memory. The patterns are often what we commonly term optical *illusions*—in this case illusions of movement in static images. Op Art paintings are simple, repetitive patterns of definite, hard-edged, often geometric shapes. In theory, such elements should not suggest movement. But the hard edges begin to blur, soften, and "swim" before our eyes. Colors vibrate and glow like neon. The flat canvas even appears to undulate and become a billowing, rippling surface. Staring for just a few moments at Bridget Riley's *Current* (**a**) reveals the way that the design seems to move and change.

Op Art works involve no recognizable subject matter, often no color, no blurred painted forms, no dynamic brushstrokes—yet the image actually *does* change. This is an illusion, of course, but an effective one. Many Op Art images can rather quickly cause optical strain. The energy-filled illusion is fascinating, but we need to look away to escape optical discomfort.

Stare at the center of the concentric circles in Tadasky's painting in **b**. Suddenly a black line begins to whirl back and forth like a propeller turning on the pattern. A dynamic element not present in the painting appears before our eyes.

a Bridget Riley. *Current.* 1964. Synthetic polymer paint on composition board, 4′10⅜″ × 4′10⅞″ (1.48 × 1.5 m). Museum of Modern Art, New York (Philip Johnson Fund).
b Tadasky. *A-101.* 1964. Synthetic polymer paint on canvas, 4′4″ (1.32 m) square. Museum of Modern Art, New York (Larry Aldrich Foundation Fund).

a

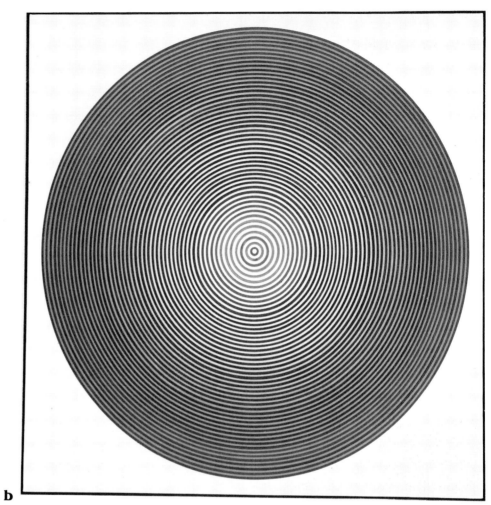

b

Mike Newman. An artist at work created on a Dicomed D38 + Design Station. 1982.

12

Design
Problem
Solving

Design Problem Solving

To a student, the word *problem* usually suggests something in a mathematics class or a science lab. Yet assignments in design classes are also often termed *problems,* and the term is apt, since art can be a problem-solving process. Art, like other careers and occupations, is concerned with seeking answers to problems. Art differs only in that its answers are visual solutions.

The arts are called "creative" fields because there are no pre-determined correct answers to the problems. Infinite variations in individual interpretation and application are possible. Problems in art vary in specifics and complexity and take various forms. Independent painters or sculptors usually create their own problems or avenues they wish to explore. These may be as wide or as narrow and limited as the artist chooses. The architect or graphic and industrial designer is usually *given* the problem, often with very specific options and clearly defined limitations. Students in art classes are also usually in this category— they execute a series of assignments devised by the instructor and requiring rather specific solutions. However, all art or visual problems are similar in that a creative solution is desired. We use the word *creative* to

---

a *Three Looms One Land: Shared Horizons.* 1982. Poster. Larry Smitherman, art director; Charles Lohrmann, designer; Noël Bennett, writer; Craddock Bagshaw, photographer; Smitherman Graphic Design, Austin, TEX.

a

Introduction

mean a solution that is original, imaginative, fresh, or unusual. This is a challenge, but many of us are creative in some area. Now this ability must be applied to the visual arts.

The creative aspect of art also includes the often heard phrase that there are "no rules" in art. This is true. In solving visual problems, there is no list of strict or absolute *do's* and *don'ts* to follow. Given all the varied objectives of visual art through the ages, definite laws are impossible. However, the phrase "no rules" may seem to imply that all designs are equally valid and visually successful. This is not true. Artistic practices and criteria have been developed from successful works, of which an artist or designer should be aware. Thus, there are guidelines (*not* rules) that will usually assist in the creation of successful designs. These guidelines certainly do not mean that the artist is limited to any specific solution.

Discussions of art often distinguish between the two aspects of *content* and *form. Content* implies the subject matter, story, or information that the artwork seeks to communicate to the viewer. *Form* is the purely visual aspect, the manipulation of the various elements and principles of design. Content is what artists want to say, form is how they say it. Problems in art can concern one or both categories.

Sometimes the aim of a work of art is purely aesthetic. Subject matter can be absent and the problem related only to creating visual pleasure. Purely abstract adornment or decoration is a very legitimate role of art. Usually problems in art do have a purpose beyond just visual satisfaction. Art is, and always has been, one means of communication. An idea or a concept can be expressed and transmitted through a visual lan-

guage. The artist or designer is *saying* something to the viewer. Here the successful solution is not only visually effective but also communicates an idea. Any of the elements of art can be used in communication. Purely abstract lines, colors, and shapes can be very effective in expressing ideas or feelings. Many times the communication is achieved through symbols, pictorial images that suggest to the viewer the theme or message. The ingenuity or creative imagination exercised in selecting these images can be important in the finished work's success.

In art as communication, images are frequently combined with written words. The advertisements we see every day usually use both elements, coordinated to reinforce the design's purpose. Countless paintings show that words are not a necessity for communication. Words can give specific information, while pictures or abstract symbols can immediately express the theme. The poster design in **a** uses both elements, but the idea is clear from only the visual elements. The dark silhouetted landscape instantly suggests the Southwest of the United States. Then the ingenious substitution of the Indian textile design for the expected sunset sky gives the theme of the exhibition.

The successful design solution in **a** is due, of course, to a good *idea.* "How do I get an idea?" is a question often heard from students. Actually, this is a dilemma that almost everyone shares from time to time. Even the professional artist can stare at the empty canvas, the successful writer at the blank page in the typewriter. An idea in art can take many forms, varying from a specific visual effect to an intellectual communication of a definite message. Ideas encompass both the areas of content and form.

It is doubtful that anyone can truly explain why or how an idea suddenly arises. While doing one thing, we can be thinking about something else. Our ideas can occur while we are in the shower, mowing the lawn, or in countless other seemingly unlikely situations. An answer to what we have been puzzling over can appear "out of the blue." But we need not be concerned here with sudden solutions. They will continue to happen, but is that the only procedure? The relevant question is, "What can we do consciously to stimulate this creative process?" What sort of activities can promote the likelihood that a solution to a problem will present itself?

Many people today are concerned with such questions. There has been a great deal of study of the "creative process," and many worthwhile books and articles are devoted to the subject. Many lengthy discussions and technical terms have evolved in this admittedly complex area. But let me suggest three very simple activities with very simple names:

Thinking
Looking
Doing

These are *not* sequential steps and certainly not independent procedures. They overlap and may be accomplished almost simultaneously or by jumping back and forth from one to another. Individuals vary; people are not programmed machines where rigid step-by-step procedures lead inevitably to answers; people's feelings and intuitions may assist in making decisions. Problems vary so that a specific assignment may immediately suggest an initial emphasis on one of these suggestions. But all three procedures can hopefully stimulate the artistic problem-solving process.

Design Problem Solving

Thinking

When confronted with a problem in any aspect of life, the usual first step is to think about it. This is applicable also to art and visual problems. Thinking is involved in all aspects of the creative process. Every step in creating a design involves choices, and the selections are determined by thinking. Chance or accident is also an element in art. But art cannot be created mindlessly, although some 20th-century art movements have attempted to eliminate rational thought as a factor in creating art and to stress intuitive or subconscious thought.

Knowing what you are doing must precede your doing it. So thinking starts with understanding the problem at hand:

Precisely what is to be achieved? What specific visual and/or intellectual effect is desired?
Are there visual stylistic requirements? (illustrative, abstraction, nonobjective, etc.)
What physical limitations are imposed? (size, color, media, etc.)
When is the solution needed?

These questions may all seem self-evident, but any time spent on solutions outside the range of these specifications will not be productive. "Failures" can occur simply because the problem was not fully understood at the very beginning.

Thinking can be especially important in art with a specific theme or message. How can the concept be communicated in visual terms? A first step is thinking logically of what images or pictures could represent this theme—and listing them or, better yet, sketching them quickly, as a visual answer is what you are seeking. Let's take a specific example:

you have a job or assignment in which the number *10* is an important element. Your job is to convey quickly and visually the idea of *10*. The written word *ten* and the numeral *10* are obvious possibilities, and you go on from there. Maybe:

the Roman numeral X
ten fingers (or toes)
a dime
a double-five domino
a tenpin (or ten of them)
two dice totalling 10
a decahedron
a playing card (ten of spades, etc.)

Each of these ideas might suggest further additions. Now expand the idea by discussing it with others. They may offer suggestions you have not considered. Professional designers often are assisted by material from market surveys showing the ideas of vast numbers of people.

One variation in thinking is called *brainstorming*. This term implies letting the mind wander freely and recording *any* idea suggested. Whether done alone or in a group, the method requires that no questions of suitability or usefulness should censor the listing of any thought that comes to mind. You literally "play" with the idea, hoping for new and unexpected images. On the theme of *ten,* perhaps:

a decimal point
$\sqrt{100}$
a boxer lying knocked out
Moses holding the Commandment tablets
the Bill of Rights

a recent Decathlon winner
a half-bottle of wine
10acity, 10ant, or Omar the 10tmaker
a ten-speed bicycle
dix, diez, dieci, zehn, etc.
and many others will occur to you

Brainstorming, by nature, produces many strange ideas, but that is the aim. In there somewhere *may* be the unique and unusual solution.

Any such list of possible images should be subjected to further thinking, exploring the appropriateness of each item or sketching it to see its visual potential. At this point, you do not necessarily decide on *one* suggestion, but narrow the very broad list to three or four worthy of further development. Here is where a consideration of the potential audience often should occur. Picking the correct symbol could depend on the future viewers. To whom is this visual message primarily addressed? college students? farmers? artists? children? retired people? the public at large? In each case the effective design symbol could be very different.

Look at the engagement party invitation in **a**. Think of the many images that can symbolize a wedding: a ring, cake, cupid, heart, bridal bouquet, and others. Here two pieces of string make profiles of the couple. Since these invitations would go to friends of the couple, this very personal symbol is highly effective. The strings at the top "tie the knot," an expression we often use to denote a wedding. The expression of an idea in visual terms designed for the intended viewers is marvelous.

a Engagement party invitation. Michael Stelzer, art director and designer; Charles Farley, writer; Noble & Associates, Springfield, MO, design firm.

Procedures

Looking

Looking is probably the primary education of any artist. An often-heard truism states that "Nature is the artist's teacher." Perhaps. Nature may be often the artist's *inspiration.* But the artist learns more by observing other art. Thus, studying art from all periods and areas is enlightening. The more familiar you are with how other artists have solved various visual problems, the better equipped you will be to find your own solution. This is true even in the negative sense of your personally rejecting a certain form or stylistic convention. Artists cannot work in a vacuum; they are concerned with, and influenced by, the past and contemporary works of others. Our advantage today (unlike the past) is that so much visual information is readily accessible through newspapers, books, and magazines. It is relatively easy for us to see how diverse artists from all geographic areas are working.

Looking is important in a more mundane sense. Whatever you are doing—walking down the street looking in store windows, leafing through a new magazine, selecting purchases in a store, visiting a local gallery, discussing student projects in class—*look* by analyzing what you see. When your attention is stopped, when the visual image is effective or dramatic, try to figure out why this is so. How was this achieved? What has attracted your attention? As an example, look at **a**. Notice not only the significance of the particular symbol for marriage chosen but also the *visual* solution. Notice the effective contrast of light vertical elements forming the profiles with the horizontal delicate italic bands of typography. A good practice is to make a quick sketch as a note of designs that seem to have a unique idea, either through symbol or visual pattern. Many artists keep clippings of effective designs in a "scrap file" to refer to for possible inspiration on future assignments.

This all describes *looking* in a general sense. Looking also includes the more formal aspect of *research.* Some projects may involve subjects of which you have little knowledge or experience. Then visual research in books or magazines limited to the specific topic is not only helpful but also necessary.

None of this implies that you *copy* or slavishly imitate another artist's work. There have been many instances in the past when art *was* taught by a precise copying of others' works or learning to paint exactly as your "master" painted. This procedure has value, but is little used today and is not what is meant here. The intention here is that you take an idea or technique and *adapt* it to your own purposes. This book is filled with illustrations showing visual ideas. Of course, your work will not be identical to any of these examples. The illustrations provide "raw material" from which you may fashion a new and original design. Ideas for a new machine or invention are protected by a patent, but this is not true of visual ideas. In this area, everyone learns from the successes (and failures) of other artists. The more you can observe and develop your critical judgment, the better it will serve you in future problem solving.

a

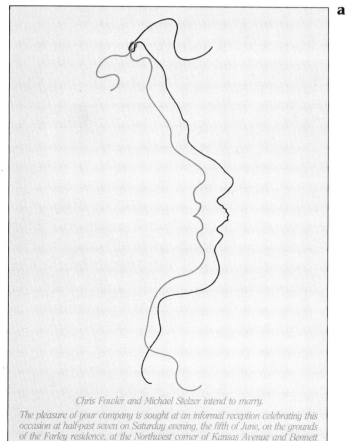

Chris Fowler and Michael Stelzer intend to marry.

The pleasure of your company is sought at an informal reception celebrating this occasion at half-past seven on Saturday evening, the fifth of June, on the grounds of the Farley residence, at the Northwest corner of Kansas Avenue and Bennett Street in Springfield, Missouri. Regrets 417/881-1492 or 869-5700. No gifts, please.

Design Problem Solving

a

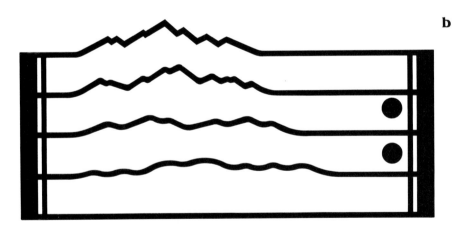

b

a Trademark for Adams Trucking. Eric Bloom, designer; Pairadice Design, Santa Cruz, CA.
b Trademark for Colorado Philharmonic Orchestra. Bob Hohnstock, art director and designer; Louie Warner, illustrator; R. L. Hohnstock & Associates, Denver, CO, agency.

Procedures

Doing

Doing may seem like a needless suggestion, as most art eventually involves the act of doing or creating the finished project. The exception is some *conceptual art* pieces, where the process can stress mainly thinking, but this is unusual. Since art is a visual field, thinking, talking, and looking constitute only the initial steps of the creative process. Sooner or later, a visual *some*thing is actually created.

What *doing* means here is to start experimenting visually, even if you have no clear direction in mind. If you are dealing with a purely visual problem (no theme, message, subject matter), then your visual experimenting should start immediately. But even with more complex problems involving concepts and symbols, actually *doing* something can stimulate the thinking aspect. Just actually *seeing* something may suggest other possibilities to you. A series of spontaneous, quickly done "roughs" (almost like a visual brainstorming) can be very helpful in deciding a direction you wish to pursue.

Sometimes artists themselves cannot tell you what exact procedure or technique gave them the solution, as the three are so closely related. The trademark designs in **a** and **b** are solutions that could well have come from a visual "playing" with possibilities.

Trademark **a** was designed for a trucking firm. The sloping slides of the capital letter *A* (the company's initial) could have visually reminded the artist of a highway seen in perspective, and a very effective design resulted.

In **b** the idea of a music festival held in the Rocky Mountains is presented in a very simple, elegant way. This trademark cleverly combines a musical staff symbol on which the lines bend to give a contour of mountains—again an idea that could have come from experimenting visually with line drawings of the two ideas.

Students often look concerned and say, "I don't know what I'm doing." This is not usually a problem or cause for worry. They are experimenting visually, and as long as they are alert as to what might (or might not) develop the process can be extremely useful. Great designs have evolved from almost unconscious doodling. After all, Columbus was confused about where he was going when he started his famous voyage.

In this whole process, experimentation is paramount. Do not settle for the first reasonable answer. Try lots of possibilities and variations, even if you eventually reject them all and return to your first idea. The exploration itself is time well spent. Your decision is now based on a choice from many possibilities, not just one or two. Of course, time limitations can be important.

Independent artists may arrive at solutions on their own time schedule; in the many fields of applied art, "deadlines" are an unhappy fact of life. Usually in the business world, only so much time can be allotted to this act of creation. Artists in these fields accept this and must budget their time accordingly. A late class project is very serious; a late project at work can cost you money or a job.

Once you have decided on a basic idea or direction, the *doing* is the primary consideration. Ideas are developed through a series of rough, rather quickly done sketches that explore various, now purely visual, solutions. Needless to say, *thinking* is still involved as you select and choose, and your previous *looking* can suggest further design possibilities. The time involved in the visual development of an idea varies from problem to problem. But very often it is helpful to get reactions—whether from a client or an instructor or even friends—during the early stages.

This whole process sounds like and is, indeed, work. Art is basically visual invention—*inventing* a creative solution to a visual problem. Remember that Thomas A. Edison defined invention as "10% *inspiration* and 90% *perspiration.*"

This design process has been nicely expressed by Josef Albers:

> To design is
> to plan and organize
> to order and relate
> and to control.
> In short it embraces
> all means opposing
> disorder and accident.
> Therefore it signifies
> a human need
> and qualifies man's
> thinking and doing.

Bibliography

Art History

Arnason, H. H. *History of Modern Art,* 2nd ed. Englewood Cliffs, N.J.: Prentice-Hall, 1976.

Elsen, Albert E. *Purposes of Art,* 3rd ed. New York: Holt, Rinehart and Winston, 1972.

Janson, H. W. *History of Art,* 2nd ed. New York: Prentice-Hall and Harry N. Abrams, Inc., 1977.

General Design

Anderson, Donald M. *Elements of Design.* New York: Holt, Rinehart and Winston, 1961.

Bevlin, Marjorie Elliott. *Design Through Discovery,* 3rd ed. New York: Holt, Rinehart and Winston, 1977.

Bothwell, Dorr, and Marlys Frey. *Notan: The Dark-Light Principle of Design.* New York: Van Nostrand Reinhold, 1976.

Carpenter, James M. *Visual Art: A Critical Introduction.* New York: Harcourt Brace Jovanovich, 1982.

Cheatham, Frank, Jane Cheatham, and Sheryl Haler. *Design Concepts and Applications.* Englewood Cliffs, N.J.: Prentice-Hall, 1983.

Collier, Graham. *Form, Space and Vision.* Englewood Cliffs, N.J.: Prentice-Hall, 1967.

De Lucio-Meyer, J. *Visual Aesthetics.* New York: Harper & Row, 1974.

De Sausmarez, Maurice. *Basic Design: The Dynamics of Visual Form.* New York: Van Nostrand Reinhold, 1975.

Faulkner, Ray, and Edwin Zeigfeld. *Art Today,* 5th ed. New York: Holt, Rinehart and Winston, 1969.

Hale, Nathan Cabot. *Abstraction in Art and Nature.* New York: Watson-Guptill Publications, 1972.

Harlan, Calvin. *Vision and Invention: A Course in Art Fundamentals.* Englewood Cliffs, N.J.: Prentice-Hall, 1970.

Henri, Robert. *The Art Spirit.* New York: Lippincott, 1960.

Hobbs, Jack A. *Art in Context,* 2nd ed. New York: Harcourt Brace Jovanovich, 1980.

Hurlburt, Allen. *Layout: The Design of the Printed Page.* New York: Watson-Guptill Publications, 1977.

————. *The Grid.* New York: Van Nostrand Reinhold, 1978.

Itten, Johannes. *Design and Form,* 2nd rev. ed. New York: Van Nostrand Reinhold, 1976.

Kepes, Gyorgy. *Language of Vision.* Chicago: Paul Theobald, 1969.

Knobler, Nathan. *The Visual Dialogue,* 2nd ed. New York: Holt, Rinehart and Winston, 1971.

Lowry, Bates. *The Visual Experience,* 2nd ed. Englewood Cliffs, N.J.: Prentice-Hall, 1975.

Maier, Manfred. *Basic Principles of Design.* New York: Van Nostrand Reinhold, 1977.

Mante, Harald. *Photo Design: Picture Composition for Black and White Photography.* New York: Van Nostrand Reinhold, 1971.

McKim, Robert H. *Thinking Visually,* rev. ed. Belmont, Calif.: Lifetime Learning Publications, 1980.

Ocvirk, Otto G., Robert O. Bone, Robert E. Stinson, and Philip R. Wigg. *Art Fundamentals: Theory and Practice,* 3rd ed. Dubuque, Iowa: William Brown, 1975.

Prohaska, Ray. *A Basic Course in Design: Introduction to Drawing and Painting,* rev. ed. Westport, Conn.: North Light, 1980.

Stoops, Jack, and Jerry Samuelson. *Design Dialogue.* Worcester, Mass.: Davis Publications, 1983.

Weismann, Donald L. *The Visual Arts as Human Experience.* Englewood Cliffs, N.J.: Prentice-Hall, 1970.

Wong, Wucius. *Principles of Two-Dimensional Design.* New York: Van Nostrand Reinhold, 1972.

————. *Principles of Three-Dimensional Design.* New York: Van Nostrand Reinhold, 1972.

Visual Perception

Arnheim, Rudolf. *Art and Visual Perception: A Psychology of the Creative Eye.* Berkeley: University of California Press, 1974.

Bloomer, Carolyn M. *Principles of Visual Perception.* New York: Van Nostrand Reinhold, 1976.

Ehrenzweig, Anton. *The Hidden Order of Art.* Berkeley: University of California Press, 1976.

Gombrich, E. H. *Art and Illusion: A Study in the Psychology of Pictorial Representation.* Princeton, N.J.: Princeton University Press, 1961.

Space

Carraher, Ronald G., and Jacqueline B. Thurston. *Optical Illusions and the Visual Arts.* New York: Van Nostrand Reinhold, 1966.

Coulin, Claudius. *Step-by-Step Perspective Drawing: For Architects, Draftsmen and Designers.* New York: Van Nostrand Reinhold, 1971.

D'Amelio, Joseph. *Perspective Drawing Handbook.* New York: Leon Amiel, Publisher, 1964.

Doblin, Jay. *Perspective: A New System for Designers,* 11th ed. New York: Whitney Library of Design, 1976.

Held, Richard, editor. *Image, Object, and Illusion,* readings from *Scientific American.* San Francisco: Freeman, 1974.

Ivins, William M. *On the Rationalization of Sight.* New York: Da Capo Press, 1973.

Luckiesh, M. *Visual Illusions: Their Causes, Characteristics and Applications.* New York: Dover Publications, 1965.

Bibliography

Mulvey, Frank. *Graphic Perception of Space.* New York: Van Nostrand Reinhold, 1969.

Pevsner, Nikolaus. *An Outline of European Architecture.* New York: Penguin Books, 1970.

Pirenne, M. H. *Optics, Painting and Photography.* Cambridge: Cambridge University Press, 1970.

Walters, Nigel V., and John Bromham. *Principles of Perspective.* New York: Watson-Guptill Publications, 1974.

White, J. *The Birth and Rebirth of Pictorial Space,* 2nd ed. New York: Harper & Row, 1973.

Texture

Battersby, Marton. *Trompe-L'oeil: The Eye Deceived.* New York: St. Martin's Press, 1974.

Brodatz, Phil. *Textures: A Photographic Album for Artists and Designers.* New York: Dover Publications, 1966.

Janis, Harriet, and Rudi Blesh. *Collage: Personalities, Concepts, Techniques,* rev. ed. Philadelphia: Chilton Book Co., 1967.

Proctor, Richard M. *The Principles of Pattern: For Craftsmen and Designers.* New York: Van Nostrand Reinhold, 1969.

Wescher, Herta. *Collage.* New York: Harry N. Abrams, 1968.

Color

Albers, Josef. *Interaction of Color,* rev. ed. New Haven, Conn.: Yale University Press, 1972.

Birren, Faber. *Creative Color: A Dynamic Approach for Artists and Designers.* New York: Van Nostrand Reinhold, 1961.

————. *Color: A Survey in Words and Pictures from Ancient Mysticism to Modern Science.* New York: University Books, 1962.

————. *Principles of Color.* New York: Van Nostrand Reinhold, 1969.

————, editor. *Itten: The Elements of Color.* New York: Van Nostrand Reinhold, 1970.

————, editor. *Munsell: A Grammar of Color.* New York: Van Nostrand Reinhold, 1969.

————. *Ostwald: The Color Primer.* New York: Van Nostrand Reinhold, 1969.

Fabri, Frank. *Color: A Complete Guide for Artists.* New York: Watson-Guptill Publications, 1967.

Gerritsen, Frank J. *Theory and Practice of Color.* New York: Van Nostrand Reinhold, 1974.

Itten, Johannes. *The Art of Color.* New York: Van Nostrand Reinhold, 1974.

Küppers, Harald. *Color: Origin, Systems, Uses.* New York: Van Nostrand Reinhold, 1973.

Rhode, Ogden N. *Modern Chromatics: The Student's Textbook of Color with Application to Art and Industry,* new ed. New York: Van Nostrand Reinhold, 1973.

Varley, Helen, editor. *Color.* Los Angeles: Knapp Press, 1980.

Verity, Enid. *Color Observed.* New York: Van Nostrand Reinhold, 1980.

Index

Photographic Sources

The author and publisher wish to thank the custodians of the works of art for supplying photographs and granting permission to use them. Unless listed below, photographs have been obtained from sources noted in the captions. References are to page number followed by illustration letter.

A/AR: Alinari/Art Resource, New York

Caisse: Caisse Nationale des Monuments Historiques et des sites, Paris

G/AR: Giraudon/Art Resource, New York

GM: Solomon R. Guggenheim Museum, New York

HB: Hedrich-Blessing, Chicago

LCG: Leo Castelli Gallery, New York

RMN: Réunion des Musées Nationaux, Paris

SJ: Sidney Janis Gallery, New York

Cover: Photo by Sheryl Gibson, Philadelphia

(x) Photo by A. F. Kersting, London; (2a) Photo by Ball-Anderson, Oakland, CA; (3b) Photo, Trustees of the Late Dame Barbara Hepworth, St. Ives, England; (5c) Photo, GM; (5d) Photo by Robert E. Mates for GM; (7d) Photo by Ben Blackwell, Oakland, CA; (9b) Photo by Ferdinand Boesch for the Pace Gallery, New York; (10c) A/AR; (14a) Photo by Robert E. Mates for GM; (14b) Photo, American Museum of Natural History, New York; (15c) Photo by A. F. Kersting, London; (17b) Photo, LCG; (17c) Photo, Bill Engdahl, HB; (22a) Photo by David Stansburg; (23b) Photo by Geoffrey Clements for SJ; (25c) G/AR; (25d) Photo, Marlborough Fine Art Ltd, London; (29c) © Bill Brandt/Photo Researchers, New York; (30b) Photo, Rheinisches Bildarchiv, Cologne, West Germany; (33c) Photo, School of Visual Arts Press, Ltd., New York; (40b) Photo, Library of Congress, Washington, DC; (41c) Photo, Spanish National Tourist Office, New York; (42a) A/AR; (45b) Photo by Ezra Stoller © ESTO, Mamaroneck, NY; (46a) G/AR; (48c) Photo, Coe Kerr Gallery, New York; (51c) Photo, Anthony d'Offay Gallery, London; (57d) G/AR; (61d) A/AR; (62a) Photo by Adolph Studly; (63c) Photo, Cohoma Riverdale Decorative Fabrics, New York; (63d) Photo by Rudolph Burckhardt, New York; (64) Photo, M. Knoedler & Co., Inc., New York; (67b) Photo, M. Knoedler & Co., Inc., New York; (68a) A/AR; (68b) G/AR; (69d) Photo by Kent Twitchell, Los Angeles; (70a) Photo by Wolfgang Volz; (73b) A/AR; (74a) Photo, Hirschl & Adler Galleries, Inc., New York; (77b) Photo, Museum of Modern Art, New York; (77c) Photo by Reinhard Friedrich, Berlin, West Germany; (80a) Photo by Peter Moore for Robert Miller Galleries, New York; (81b) Photo by Carmelo Guadagno for GM; (84c) A/AR; (93d) A/AR; (95b) Photo by Jeffrey Nintzel; (96a) Photo by George Gardner; (96b) Photo by George Gardner; (97c) Sopraintendenza per i Beni Artistici e Storici, Parma e Piacenza, Italy; (107d) Photo, Sovfoto, New York; (116a) Photo, American School of Classical Studies, Athens, Greece: Agora Excavations; (116b) Photo, Australian Information Service, New York; (117c) Photo, Terry Dintenfass Gallery, New York; (124b) Photo by Norman McGrath, New York; (129e) G/AR; (132a) RMN; (134d) Photo, Werner Kramarsky, New York; (136a) Photo by Eric Pollitzer, Hempstead, NY; (136b) A/AR; (136c) Photo by Rudolph Burckhardt for LCG; (140c) Bildarchiv Preussischer Kulturbesiltz, Berlin, West Germany; (144a) Photo, Noortman & Brod, London; (146a) Photos by Bernd Kirtz, Duisburg, West Germany; (146b) Photo by Geoffrey Clements for Paula Cooper Gallery, New York; (149b) Photo, Bulloz, Paris; (149d) Photo, David Anderson Gallery, New York; (150b) A/AR; (151c) Photo by Errol Rainness; (152a) A/AR; (153e) Smithsonian Institution Photo NO 83-10907; (154a) Photo by Carmelo Guardagno for GM; (155b) Photo by Geoffrey Clements for SJ; (156b) Photo, Gerald & Cullen Rapp, Inc., New York; (156c) Photo, LCG; (157e) Photo by Louie Psihoyos, Contact Press Images, New York; (161c) Photo by The Colour Company, Denver; (163c) Photo, National Gallery, London; (163d) G/AR; (164b) From *The Composing Room, About Us.* 1960; (169b) Photo by Ezra Stoller © ESTO, Mamaroneck, NY; (171c) Photo by Carmelo Guadagno for GM; (173c) Photo by Rudolph Burckhardt for LCG; (176c) Photo by Marilyn Levine, O. K. Harris Gallery, New York; (178a) Photo, Schumacher, New York; (186a) G/AR; (189c) Photo by Ralph Kleinhempel, Hamburg, West Germany; (195c) Photo by Leonard von Matt, Buochs, Switzerland; (195d) Photo, Otto Stangl Galerie, Munich, West Germany; (197c) Photo by Marlen Perez, Museum Bellerive, Zurich; (199c) Photo by Howard Millard, Pelham, NY; (202b) Photo, Wildenstein & Co., New York; (203d) Photo, Marlborough Fine Art Ltd., London; (208b) Photo by Carmelo Guadagno & David Heald for GM; (210a) G/AR; (211c) Photo, Gimpel & Weitzenhoffer, Ltd., New York; (218a) Caisse; (220a) Caisse; (223b) Istituto-Centrale per il Catalogo e la Documentazione, Rome; (223d) A/AR; (224a) Photo by Elliott Erwitt, Magnum Photos, New York; (225d) Photo by Carmelo Guadagno for GM; (226b) RMN; (227d) A/AR; (228a) Bayerische Staatsgemälde Sammlungen, Munich, West Germany; (228b) Photo by Carmelo Guadagno for GM

Works by Klee; Schwitters: © Cosmopress, Geneva & ADAGP, Paris/VAGA, New York, 1985

Works by Cassatt; Corneille/Beverloo; Dubuffet; Duchamp; Kandinsky; Kupka; Lurçat; Magritte; Miro; Soulages; Tàpies: © ADAGP, Paris/VAGA, New York, 1985

Works by Escher; Mondrian: © Beeldrecht, Amsterdam/VAGA, New York, 1985

Works by Bonnard; Dali; Ernst; Gris; Le Corbusier; Matisse; Picasso; Vasarely; Renoir; Rouault; Soutine; Utrillo: © SPADEM, Paris/VAGA, New York, 1985

Work by Grosz: © Bild-Kunst, West Germany/Estate of George Grosz/VAGA, New York, 1985

Works by © Robert Rauschenberg/; © Andy Warhol/; © Clayton Pond/; © Larry Rivers/; © Estate of Grant Wood/; © Estate of David Smith/; © Roy Lichtenstein/; VAGA, New York, 1985